HOME UNIVERSITY LIBRARY
OF MODERN KNOWLEDGE

No. 69

A complete classified list of the volumes of THE HOME UNIVERSITY LIBRARY *already published will be found at the back of this book.*

A HISTORY
OF FREEDOM OF
THOUGHT

BY

J. B. BURY, M.A., F.B.A.

HON. D.LITT. OF OXFORD, DURHAM, AND DUBLIN, AND
HON. LL.D. OF EDINBURGH, GLASGOW, AND ABERDEEN
UNIVERSITIES ; REGIUS PROFESSOR OF MODERN
HISTORY, CAMBRIDGE UNIVERSITY
AUTHOR OF "HISTORY OF THE LATER ROMAN EMPIRE"
"HISTORY OF GREECE," "HISTORY OF THE
EASTERN ROMAN EMPIRE," ETC.

NEW YORK
HENRY HOLT AND COMPANY
LONDON
WILLIAMS AND NORGATE

would upset the established order of this familiar world. A new idea, inconsistent with some of the beliefs which he holds, means the necessity of rearranging his mind; and this process is laborious, requiring a painful expenditure of brain-energy. To him and his fellows, who form the vast majority, new ideas, and opinions which cast doubt on established beliefs and institutions, seem evil because they are disagreeable.

The repugnance due to mere mental laziness is increased by a positive feeling of fear. The conservative instinct hardens into the conservative doctrine that the foundations of society are endangered by any alterations in the structure. It is only recently that men have been abandoning the belief that the welfare of a state depends on rigid stability and on the preservation of its traditions and institutions unchanged. Wherever that belief prevails, novel opinions are felt to be dangerous as well as annoying, and any one who asks inconvenient questions about the why and the wherefore of accepted principles is considered a pestilent person.

The conservative instinct, and the conservative doctrine which is its consequence, are strengthened by superstition. If the social structure, including the whole body of customs and opinions, is associated intimately with religious belief and is supposed to be under divine patronage, criticism of the social order savours of impiety, while criticism of the religious belief is a direct challenge to the wrath of supernatural powers.

The psychological motives which produce a conservative spirit hostile to new ideas are reinforced by the active opposition of certain powerful sections of the community, such as a class, a caste, or a priesthood, whose interests are bound up with the maintenance of the established order and the ideas on which it rests.

Let us suppose, for instance, that a people believes that solar eclipses are signs employed by their Deity for the special purpose of communicating useful information to them, and that a clever man discovers the true cause of eclipses. His compatriots in the first place dislike his discovery because they find it very difficult to reconcile with their other ideas; in the second place, it disturbs them, because it uspets an arrangement which they consider highly advantageous to their community; finally, it frightens them, as an offence to their Divinity. The priests, one of whose functions is to interpret the divine signs, are alarmed and enraged at a doctrine which menaces their power.

In prehistoric days, these motives, operating strongly, must have made change slow in communities which progressed, and hindered some communities from progressing at all. But they have continued to operate more or less throughout history, obstructing knowledge and progress. We can observe them at work to-day even in the most advanced societies, where they have no longer the power to arrest development or repress the publication of revolutionary opinions. We still meet people who consider a new idea an annoyance and probably a danger. Of those to whom socialism is repugnant, how many are there who have never examined the arguments for and against it, but turn away in disgust simply because the notion disturbs their mental universe and implies a drastic criticism on the order of things to which they are accustomed? And how many are there who would refuse to consider any proposals for altering our imperfect matrimonial institutions, because such an idea offends a mass of prejudice associated with religious sanctions? They may be right or not, but if they are, it is not their fault. They are actuated by the same motives which were a bar to progress in primitive societies. The existence of people of this mentality, reared in an atmosphere of freedom, side by side with others who are always looking out for new ideas and regretting that there are not more about, enables us to realize how, when public opinion was formed by the views of such men, thought was fettered and the impediments to knowledge enormous.

Although the liberty to publish one's opinions on any subject without regard to authority or the prejudices of one's neighbours is now a well-established principle, I imagine that only the minority of those who would be ready to fight to the death rather than surrender it could defend it on rational grounds. We are apt to take for granted that freedom of speech is a natural and inalienable birthright of man, and perhaps to think that this is a sufficient answer to all that can be said on the other side. But it is difficult to see how such a right can be established.

If a man has any "natural rights," the right to preserve his life and the right to reproduce his kind are certainly such. Yet human societies impose upon their members restrictions in the exercise of both these rights. A starving man is prohibited from taking food which belongs to somebody else. Promiscuous reproduction is restricted by various laws or customs. It is admitted that society is justified in restricting these elementary rights, because without such restrictions an ordered society could not exist. If then we concede that the expression of opinion is a right of the same kind, it is impossible to contend that on this ground it can claim immunity from interference or that society acts unjustly in regulating it. But the concession is too large. For whereas in the other cases the limitations affect the conduct of every one, restrictions on freedom of opinion affect only the comparatively small number who have any opinions, revolutionary or unconventional, to express. The truth is that no valid argument can be founded on the conception of natural rights, because it involves an untenable theory of the relations between society and its members.

On the other hand, those who have the responsibility of governing a society can argue that it is as incumbent on them to prohibit the circulation of pernicious opinions as to prohibit any anti-social actions. They can argue that a man may do far more harm by propagating anti-social doctrines than by stealing his neighbour's horse or making love to his neighbour's wife. They are responsible for the welfare of the State, and if they are convinced that an opinion is dangerous, by menacing the political, religious, or moral assumptions on which the society is based, it is their duty to protect society against it, as against any other danger.

The true answer to this argument for limiting freedom of thought will appear in due course. It was far from obvious. A long time was needed to arrive at the conclusion that coercion of opinion is a mistake, and only a part of the world is yet convinced. That conclusion, so far as I can judge, is the most important ever reached by men. It was the issue of a continuous struggle between authority and reason—the subject of this volume. The word *authority* requires some comment.

If you ask somebody how he knows something, he may say, "I have it on good authority," or, "I read it in a book," or, "It is a matter of common knowledge," or, "I learned it at school." Any of these replies means that he has accepted information from others, trusting in their knowledge, without verifying their statements or thinking the matter out for himself. And the greater part of most men's knowledge and beliefs is of this kind, taken without verification from their parents, teachers, acquaintances, books, newspapers. When an English boy learns French, he takes the conjugations and the meanings of the words on the authority of his teacher or his grammar. The fact that in a certain place, marked on the map, there is a populous city called Calcutta, is for most

the conflict, authority has had great advantages. At any time the people who really care about reason have been a small minority, and probably will be so for a long time to come. Reason's only weapon has been argument. Authority has employed physical and moral violence, legal coercion and social displeasure. Sometimes she has attempted to use the sword of her adversary, thereby wounding herself. Indeed the weakest point in the strategical position of authority was that her champions, being human, could not help making use of reasoning processes and the result was that they were divided among themselves. This gave reason her chance. Operating, as it were, in the enemy's camp and professedly in the enemy's cause, she was preparing her own victory.

It may be objected that there is a legitimate domain for authority, consisting of doctrines which lie outside human experience and therefore cannot be proved or verified, but at the same time cannot be disproved. Of course, any number of propositions can be invented which cannot be disproved, and it is open to any one who possesses exuberant faith to believe them; but no one will maintain that they all deserve credence so long as their falsehood is not demonstrated. And if only some deserve credence, who, except reason, is to decide which? If the reply is, Authority, we are confronted by the difficulty that many beliefs backed by authority have been finally disproved and are universally abandoned. Yet some people speak as if we were not justified in rejecting a theological doctrine unless we can prove it false. But the burden of proof does not lie upon the rejecter. I remember a conversation in which, when some disrespectful remark was made about hell, a loyal friend of that establishment said triumphantly, "But, absurd as it may seem, you cannot disprove it." If you were told that in a certain planet revolving round Sirius there is a race of donkeys who talk the English language and spend their time in discussing eugenics, you could not disprove the statement, but would it, on that account, have any claim to be believed? Some minds would be prepared to accept it, if it were reiterated often enough, through the potent force of suggestion. This force, exercised largely by emphatic repetition (the theoretical basis, as has been observed, of the modern practice of advertising), has played a great part in establishing authoritative opinions and propagating religious creeds. Reason fortunately is able to avail herself of the same help.

The following sketch is confined to Western

civilization. It begins with Greece and attempts to indicate the chief phases. It is the merest introduction to a vast and intricate subject, which, treated adequately, would involve not only the history of religion, of the Churches, of heresies, of persecution, but also the history of philosophy, of the natural sciences and of political theories. From the sixteenth century to the French Revolution nearly all important historical events bore in some way on the struggle for freedom of thought. It would require a lifetime to calculate, and many books to describe, all the directions and interactions of the intellectual and social forces which, since the fall of ancient civilization, have hindered and helped the emancipation of reason. All one can do, all one could do even in a much bigger volume than this, is to indicate the general course of the struggle and dwell on some particular aspects which the writer may happen to have specially studied.

CHAPTER II

REASON FREE

(GREECE AND ROME)

WHEN we are asked to specify the debt which civilization owes to the Greeks, their

achievements in literature and art naturally
occur to us first of all. But a truer answer
may be that our deepest gratitude is due to
them as the originators of liberty of thought
and discussion. For this freedom of spirit
was not only the condition of their speculations in philosophy, their progress in science,
their experiments in political institutions; it
was also a condition of their literary and artistic excellence. Their literature, for instance, could not have been what it is if they
had been debarred from free criticism of life.
But apart from what they actually accom-
plished, even if they had not achieved the
wonderful things they did in most of the
realms of human activity, their assertion of
the principle of liberty would place them in
the highest rank among the benefactors of the
race; for it was one of the greatest steps in
human progress.

We do not know enough about the earliest
history of the Greeks to explain how it was
that they attained their free outlook upon
the world and came to possess the will and
courage to set no bounds to the range of their
criticism and curiosity. We have to take
this character as a fact. But it must be remembered that the Greeks consisted of a large
number of separate peoples, who varied
largely in temper, customs and traditions,

though they had important features common to all. Some were conservative, or backward, or unintellectual compared with others. In this chapter "the Greeks" does not mean all the Greeks, but only those who count most in the history of civilization, especially the Ionians and Athenians.

Ionia in Asia Minor was the cradle of free speculation. The history of European science and European philosophy begins in Ionia. Here (in the sixth and fifth centuries B.C.) the early philosophers by using their reason sought to penetrate into the origin and structure of the world. They could not of course free their minds entirely from received notions, but they began the work of destroying orthodox views and religious faiths. Xenophanes may specially be named among these pioneers of thought (though he was not the most important or the ablest), because the toleration of his teaching illustrates the freedom of the atmosphere in which these men lived. He went about from city to city, calling in question on moral grounds the popular beliefs about the gods and goddesses, and ridiculing the anthropomorphic conceptions which the Greeks had formed of their divinities. "If oxen had hands and the capacities of men, they would make gods in the shape of oxen." This attack on received theology was an attack on the veracity of the old poets, especially Homer, who was considered the highest authority on mythology. Xenophanes criticized him severely for ascribing to the gods acts which, committed by men, would be considered highly disgraceful. We do not hear that any attempt was made to restrain him from thus assailing traditional beliefs and branding Homer as immoral. We must remember that the Homeric poems were never supposed to be the word of God. It has been said that Homer was the Bible of the Greeks. The remark exactly misses the truth. The Greeks fortunately had no Bible, and this fact was both an expression and an important condition of their freedom. Homer's poems were secular, not religious, and it may be noted that they are freer from immorality and savagery than sacred books that one could mention. Their authority was immense; but it was not binding like the authority of a sacred book, and so Homeric criticism was never hampered like Biblical criticism.

In this connexion, notice may be taken of another expression and condition of freedom, the absence of sacerdotalism. The priests of the temples never became powerful castes, tyrannizing over the community in their own interests and able to silence voices raised against religious beliefs. The civil authorities kept the general control of public worship in their own hands, and, if some priestly families might have considerable influence, yet as a rule the priests were virtually State servants whose voice carried no weight except concerning the technical details of ritual.

To return to the early philosophers, who were mostly materialists, the record of their speculations is an interesting chapter in the history of rationalism. Two great names may be selected, Heraclitus and Democritus, because they did more perhaps than any of the others, by sheer hard thinking, to train reason to look upon the universe in new ways and to shock the unreasoned conceptions of common sense. It was startling to be taught, for the first time, by Heraclitus, that the appearance of stability and permanence which material things present to our senses is a false appearance, and that the world and everything in it are changing every instant. Democritus performed the amazing feat of working out an atomic theory of the universe, which was revived in the seventeenth century and is connected, in the history of speculation, with the most modern physical and chemical theories of matter. No fantastic tales of creation, imposed by sacred authority, hampered these powerful brains.

All this philosophical speculation prepared

the way for the educationalists who were
known as the Sophists. They begin to appear
after the middle of the fifth century. They
worked here and there throughout Greece,
constantly travelling, training young men for
public life, and teaching them to use their
reason. As educators they had practical ends
in view. They turned away from the problems of the physical universe to the problems
of human life—morality and politics. Here
they were confronted with the difficulty of
distinguishing between truth and error, and
the ablest of them investigated the nature
of knowledge, the method of reason—logic—
and the instrument of reason—speech. Whatever their particular theories might be, their
general spirit was that of free inquiry and
discussion. They sought to test everything
by reason. The second half of the fifth century might be called the age of Illumination.

It may be remarked that the knowledge
of foreign countries which the Greeks had
acquired had a considerable effect in promoting a sceptical attitude towards authority.
When a man is acquainted only with the
habits of his own country, they seem so much
a matter of course that he ascribes them to
nature, but when he travels abroad and finds
totally different habits and standards of
conduct prevailing, he begins to understand

the power of custom; and learns that morality and religion are matters of latitude. This discovery tends to weaken authority, and to raise disquieting reflections, as in the case of one who, brought up as a Christian, comes to realize that, if he had been born on the Ganges or the Euphrates, he would have firmly believed in entirely different dogmas.

Of course these movements of intellectual freedom were, as in all ages, confined to the minority. Everywhere the masses were exceedingly superstitious. They believed that the safety of their cities depended on the good-will of their gods. If this superstitious spirit were alarmed, there was always a danger that philosophical speculations might be persecuted. And this occurred in Athens. About the middle of the fifth century Athens had not only become the most powerful State in Greece, but was also taking the highest place in literature and art. She was a full-fledged democracy. Political discussion was perfectly free. At this time she was guided by the statesman Pericles, who was personally a freethinker, or at least was in touch with all the subversive speculations of the day. He was especially intimate with the philosopher Anaxagoras who had come from Ionia to teach at Athens. In regard to the popular gods Anaxagoras was a thorough-

going unbeliever. The political enemies of
Pericles struck at him by attacking his friend.
They introduced and carried a blasphemy
law, to the effect that unbelievers and those
who taught theories about the celestial world
might be impeached. It was easy to prove
that Anaxagoras was a blasphemer who
taught that the gods were abstractions and
that the sun, to which the ordinary Athenian
said prayers morning and evening, was a mass
of flaming matter. The influence of Pericles
saved him from death; he was heavily fined
and left Athens for Lampsacus, where he was
treated with consideration and honour.

Other cases are recorded which show that
anti-religious thought was liable to be persecuted. Protagoras, one of the greatest of the
Sophists, published a book *On the Gods*,
the object of which seems to have been to
prove that one cannot know the gods by
reason. The first words ran: "Concerning
the gods, I cannot say that they exist nor
yet that they do not exist. There are more
reasons than one why we cannot know.
There is the obscurity of the subject and there
is the brevity of human life." A charge of
blasphemy was lodged against him and he fled
from Athens. But there was no systematic
policy of suppressing free thought. Copies
of the work of Protagoras were collected and

burned, but the book of Anaxagoras setting forth the views for which he had been condemned was for sale on the Athenian bookstalls at a popular price. Rationalistic ideas moreover were venturing to appear on the stage, though the dramatic performances, at the feasts of the god Dionysus, were religious solemnities. The poet Euripides was saturated with modern speculation, and, while different opinions may be held as to the tendencies of some of his tragedies, he often allows his characters to express highly unorthodox views. He was prosecuted for impiety by a popular politician. We may suspect that during the last thirty years of the fifth century unorthodoxy spread considerably among the educated classes. There was a large enough section of influential rationalists to render impossible any organized repression of liberty, and the chief evil of the blasphemy law was that it could be used for personal or party reasons. Some of the prosecutions, about which we know, were certainly due to such motives, others may have been prompted by genuine bigotry and by the fear lest sceptical thought should extend beyond the highly educated and leisured class. It was a generally accepted principle among the Greeks, and afterwards among the Romans, that religion was a good and necessary thing

for the common people. Men who did not
believe in its truth believed in its usefulness
as a political institution, and as a rule philosophers did not seek to diffuse disturbing
"truth" among the masses. It was the custom, much more than at the present day, for
those who did not believe in the established
cults to conform to them externally. Popular higher education was not an article in the
programme of Greek statesmen or thinkers.
And perhaps it may be argued that in the
circumstances of the ancient world it would
have been hardly practicable.

There was, however, one illustrious Athenian, who thought differently—Socrates, the
philosopher. Socrates was the greatest of
the educationalists, but unlike the others he
taught gratuitously, though he was a poor
man. His teaching always took the form of
discussion; the discussion often ended in no
positive result, but had the effect of showing
that some received opinion was untenable
and that truth is difficult to ascertain. He
had indeed certain definite views about
knowledge and virtue, which are of the
highest importance in the history of philosophy, but for our present purpose his significance lies in his enthusiasm for discussion and criticism. He taught those with
whom he conversed—and he conversed in-

discriminately with all who would listen to
him—to bring all popular beliefs before the
bar of reason, to approach every inquiry
with an open mind, and not to judge by the
opinion of majorities or the dictate of authority; in short to seek for other tests of the
truth of an opinion than the fact that it is
held by a great many people. Among his
disciples were all the young men who were to
become the leading philosophers of the next
generation and some who played prominent
parts in Athenian history.

If the Athenians had had a daily press,
Socrates would have been denounced by the
journalists as a dangerous person. They had
a comic drama, which constantly held up to
ridicule philosophers and sophists and their
vain doctrines. We possess one play (the
Clouds of Aristophanes) in which Socrates
is pilloried as a typical representative of
impious and destructive speculations. Apart
from annoyances of this kind, Socrates
reached old age, pursuing the task of instruct-
ing his fellow-citizens, without any evil
befalling him. Then, at the age of seventy,
he was prosecuted as an atheist and corrupter
of youth and was put to death (399 B.C.).
It is strange that if the Athenians really
thought him dangerous they should have
suffered him so long. There can, I think, be

little doubt that the motives of the accusation were political.[1] Socrates, looking at things as he did, could not be sympathetic with unlimited democracy, or approve of the principle that the will of the ignorant majority was a good guide. He was probably known to sympathize with those who wished to limit the franchise. When, after a struggle in which the constitution had been more than once overthrown, democracy emerged triumphant (403 B.C.), there was a bitter feeling against those who had not been its friends, and of these disloyal persons Socrates was chosen as a victim. If he had wished, he could easily have escaped. If he had given an undertaking to teach no more, he would almost certainly have been acquitted. As it was, of the 501 ordinary Athenians who were his judges, a very large minority voted for his acquittal. Even then, if he had adopted a different tone, he would not have been condemned to death.

He rose to the great occasion and vindicated freedom of discussion in a wonderful unconventional speech. The *Apology of Socrates*, which was composed by his most brilliant pupil, Plato the philosopher, repro-

[1] This has been shown very clearly by Professor Jackson in the article on "Socrates" in the *Encyclopædia Britannica*, last edition.

duces the general tenor of his defence. It is clear that he was not able to meet satisfactorily the charge that he did not acknowledge the gods worshipped by the city, and his explanations on this point are the weak part of his speech. But he met the accusation that he corrupted the minds of the young by a splendid plea for free discussion. This is the most valuable section of the *Apology;* it is as impressive to-day as ever. I think the two principal points which he makes are these—

(1) He maintains that the individual should at any cost refuse to be coerced by any human authority or tribunal into a course which his own mind condemns as wrong. That is, he asserts *the supremacy of the individual conscience,* as we should say, over human law. He represents his own life-work as a sort of religious quest; he feels convinced that in devoting himself to philosophical discussion he has done the bidding of a super-human guide; and he goes to death rather than be untrue to this personal conviction. "If you propose to acquit me," he says, "on condition that I abandon my search for truth, I will say: I thank you, O Athenians, but I will obey God, who, as I believe, set me this task, rather than you, and so long as I have breath and strength I will never

cease from my occupation with philosophy.
I will continue the practice of accosting
whomever I meet and saying to him, 'Are
you not ashamed of setting your heart on
wealth and honours while you have no care
for wisdom and truth and making your soul
better?' I know not what death is—it may
be a good thing, and I am not afraid of it.
But I do know that it is a bad thing to desert
one's post and I prefer what may be good to
what I know to be bad."

(2) He insists on *the public value of free
discussion*. "In me you have a stimulating
critic, persistently urging you with persuasion
and reproaches, persistently testing your
opinions and trying to show you that you are
really ignorant of what you suppose you
know. Daily discussion of the matters about
which you hear me conversing is the highest
good for man. Life that is not tested by such
discussion is not worth living."

Thus in what we may call the earliest
justification of liberty of thought we have
two significant claims affirmed: the inde-
feasible right of the conscience of the individual—a claim on which later struggles
for liberty were to turn; and the social
importance of discussion and criticism. The
former claim is not based on argument but
on intuition; it rests in fact on the assump-

tion of some sort of superhuman moral principle, and to those who, not having the same personal experience as Socrates, reject this assumption, his pleading does not carry weight. The second claim, after the experience of more than 2,000 years, can be formulated more comprehensively now with bearings of which he did not dream.

The circumstances of the trial of Socrates illustrate both the tolerance and the intolerance which prevailed at Athens. His long immunity, the fact that he was at last indicted from political motives and perhaps personal also, the large minority in his favour, all show that thought was normally free, and that the mass of intolerance which existed was only fitfully invoked, and perhaps most often to serve other purposes. I may mention the case of the philosopher Aristotle, who some seventy years later left Athens because he was menaced by a prosecution for blasphemy, the charge being a pretext for attacking one who belonged to a certain political party. The persecution of opinion was never organized.

It may seem curious that to find the persecuting spirit in Greece we have to turn to the philosophers. Plato, the most brilliant disciple of Socrates, constructed in his later years an ideal State. In this State he instituted a religion considerably different from the current religion, and proposed to compel all the citizens to believe in his gods on pain of death or imprisonment. All freedom of discussion was excluded under the cast-iron system which he conceived. But the point of interest in his attitude is that he did not care much whether a religion was true, but only whether it was morally useful; he was prepared to promote morality by edifying fables; and he condemned the popular mythology not because it was false, but because it did not make for righteousness.

The outcome of the large freedom permitted at Athens was a series of philosophies which had a common source in the conversations of Socrates. Plato, Aristotle, the Stoics, the Epicureans, the Sceptics—it may be maintained that the efforts of thought represented by these names have had a deeper influence on the progress of man than any other continuous intellectual movement, at least until the rise of modern science in a new epoch of liberty.

The doctrines of the Epicureans, Stoics, and Sceptics all aimed at securing peace and guidance for the individual soul. They were widely propagated throughout the Greek world from the third century B.C., and we may say that from this time onward most

authority. Socrates had seen that laws may
be unjust and that peoples may go wrong,
but he had found no principle for the guidance of society. The Stoics discovered it in
the law of nature, prior and superior to all
the customs and written laws of peoples, and
this doctrine, spreading outside Stoic circles,
caught hold of the Roman world and affected
Roman legislation.

These philosophies have carried us from
Greece to Rome. In the later Roman Republic and the early Empire, no restrictions
were imposed on opinion, and these philosophies, which made the individual the first
consideration, spread widely. Most of the
leading men were unbelievers in the official
religion of the State, but they considered it
valuable for the purpose of keeping the uneducated populace in order. A Greek historian expresses high approval of the Roman
policy of cultivating superstition for the
benefit of the masses. This was the attitude
of Cicero, and the view that a false religion
is indispensable as a social machine was general among ancient unbelievers. It is common,
in one form or another, to-day; at least, religions are constantly defended on the ground
not of truth but of utility. This defence belongs to the statecraft of Machiavelli, who
taught that religion is necessary for govern-

ment, and that it may be the duty of a ruler to support a religion which he believes to be false.

A word must be said of Lucian (second century A.D.), the last Greek man of letters whose writings appeal to everybody. He attacked the popular mythology with open ridicule. It is impossible to say whether his satires had any effect at the time beyond affording enjoyment to educated infidels who read them. *Zeus in a Tragedy Part* is one of the most effective. The situation which Lucian imagined here would be paralleled if a modern writer were blasphemously to represent the Persons of the Trinity with some eminent angels and saints discussing in a celestial smoke-room the alarming growth of unbelief in England and then by means of a telephonic apparatus overhearing a dispute between a freethinker and a parson on a public platform in London. The absurdities of anthropomorphism have never been the subject of more brilliant jesting than in Lucian's satires.

The general rule of Roman policy was to tolerate throughout the Empire all religions and all opinions. Blasphemy was not punished. The principle was expressed in the maxim of the Emperor Tiberius: "If the gods are insulted, let them see to it themselves." An exception to the rule of tolerance was made in the case of the Christian sect, and the treatment of this Oriental religion may be said to have inaugurated religious persecution in Europe. It is a matter of interest to understand why Emperors who were able, humane, and not in the least fanatical, adopted this exceptional policy.

For a long time the Christians were only known to those Romans who happened to hear of them, as a sect of the Jews. The Jewish was the one religion which, on account of its exclusiveness and intolerance, was regarded by the tolerant pagans with disfavour and suspicion. But though it sometimes came into collision with the Roman authorities and some ill-advised attacks upon it were made, it was the constant policy of the Emperors to let it alone and to protect the Jews against the hatred which their own fanaticism aroused. But while the Jewish religion was endured so long as it was confined to those who were born into it, the prospect of its dissemination raised a new question. Grave misgivings might arise in the mind of a ruler at seeing a creed spreading which was aggressively hostile to all the other creeds of the world—creeds which lived together in amity—and had earned for its adherents the reputation of being the enemies of the human race. Might not its expansion

beyond the Israelites involve ultimately a
danger to the Empire?   For its spirit was incompatible with the traditions and basis of
Roman society.   The Emperor Domitian
seems to have seen the question in this light,
and he took severe measures to hinder the
proselytizing of Roman citizens.   Some of
those whom he struck may have been Christians, but if he was aware of the distinction,
there was from his point of view no difference.
Christianity resembled Judaism, from which
it sprang, in intolerance and in hostility
towards Roman society, but it differed by
the fact that it made many proselytes while
Judaism made few.

Under Trajan we find that the principle
has been laid down that to be a Christian is
an offence punishable by death.   Hencefor-
ward Christianity remained an illegal religion.
But in practice the law was not applied rig-
orously or logically.   The Emperors desired,
if possible, to extirpate Christianity without shedding blood.   Trajan laid down that
Christians were not to be sought out, that no
anonymous charges were to be noticed, and
that an informer who failed to make good
his charge should be liable to be punished
under the laws against calumny.   Christians themselves recognized that this edict
practically protected them.   There were

some executions in the second century—not
many that are well attested—and Christians
courted the pain and glory of martyrdom.
There is evidence to show that when they
were arrested their escape was often connived
at. In general, the persecution of the Christians was rather provoked by the populace
than desired by the authorities. The populace felt a horror of this mysterious Oriental
sect which openly hated all the gods and
prayed for the destruction of the world.
When floods, famines, and especially fires
occurred they were apt to be attributed to the
black magic of the Christians.

When any one was accused of Christianity,
he was required, as a means of testing the
truth of the charge, to offer incense to the
gods or to the statues of deified Emperors.
His compliance at once exonerated him. The
objection of the Christians—they and the
Jews were the only objectors—to the worship
of the Emperors was, in the eyes of the
Romans, one of the most sinister signs that
their religion was dangerous. The purpose
of this worship was to symbolize the unity
and solidarity of an Empire which embraced
so many peoples of different beliefs and
different gods; its intention was political,
to promote union and loyalty; and it is not
surprising that those who denounced it should

be suspected of a disloyal spirit. But it must be noted that there was no necessity for any citizen to take part in this worship. No conformity was required from any inhabitants of the Empire who were not serving the State as soldiers or civil functionaries. Thus the effect was to debar Christians from military and official careers.

The Apologies for Christianity which appeared at this period (second century) might have helped, if the Emperors (to whom some of them were addressed) had read them, to confirm the view that it was a political danger. It would have been easy to read between the lines that, if the Christians ever got the upper hand, they would not spare the cults of the State. The contemporary work of Tatian (*A Discourse to the Greeks*) reveals what the Apologists more or less sought to disguise, invincible hatred towards the civilization in which they lived. Any reader of the Christian literature of the time could not fail to see that in a State where Christians had the power there would be no tolerance of other religious practices.[1] If the Emperors made an exception to their tolerant policy in the case of Christianity, their purpose was to safeguard tolerance.

[1] For the evidence of the Apologists see A. Bouché-Leclercq, *Religious Intolerance and Politics* (French, 1911) —a valuable review of the whole subject.

In the third century the religion, though still forbidden, was quite openly tolerated; the Church organized itself without concealment; ecclesiastical councils assembled without interference. There were some brief and local attempts at repression, there was only one grave persecution (begun by Decius, A.D. 250, and continued by Valerian). In fact, throughout this century, there were not many victims, though afterwards the Christians invented a whole mythology of martyrdoms. Many cruelties were imputed to Emperors under whom we know that the Church enjoyed perfect peace.

A long period of civil confusion, in which the Empire seemed to be tottering to its fall, had been terminated by the Emperor Diocletian, who, by his radical administrative reforms, helped to preserve the Roman power in its integrity for another century. He desired to support his work of political consolidation by reviving the Roman spirit, and he attempted to infuse new life into the official religion. To this end he determined to suppress the growing influence of the Christians, who, though a minority, were very numerous, and he organized a persecution. It was long, cruel and bloody; it was the most whole-hearted, general and systematic effort to crush the forbidden faith. It was a failure, the Christians were now too numerous to be crushed. After the abdication of Diocletian, the Emperors who reigned in different parts of the realm did not agree as to the expediency of his policy, and the persecution ended by edicts of toleration (A.D. 311 and 313). These documents have an interest for the history of religious liberty.

The first, issued in the eastern provinces, ran as follows:—

"We were particularly desirous of reclaiming into the way of reason and nature the deluded Christians, who had renounced the religion and ceremonies instituted by their fathers and, presumptuously despising the practice of antiquity, had invented extravagant laws and opinions according to the dictates of their fancy, and had collected a various society from the different provinces of our Empire. The edicts which we have published to enforce the worship of the gods, having exposed many of the Christians to danger and distress, many having suffered death and many more, who still persist in their impious folly, being left destitute of *any* public exercise of religion, we are disposed to extend to those unhappy men the effects of our wonted clemency. We permit them, therefore, freely to profess their private opinions, and to assemble in their conventicles without fear or molestation, provided always that they preserve a due respect to the established laws and government." [1]

The second, of which Constantine was the author, known as the Edict of Milan, was to a similar effect, and based toleration on the Emperor's care for the peace and happiness of his subjects and on the hope of appeasing the Deity whose seat is in heaven.

The relations between the Roman government and the Christians raised the general question of persecution and freedom of conscience. A State, with an official religion, but perfectly tolerant of all creeds and cults, finds that a society had arisen in its midst which is uncompromisingly hostile to all creeds but its own and which, if it had the power, would suppress all but its own. The government, in self-defence, decides to check the dissemination of these subversive ideas and makes the profession of that creed a crime, not on account of its particular tenets, but on account of the social consequences of those tenets. The members of the society cannot without violating their consciences and incurring damnation abandon their exclusive doctrine. The principle of freedom of conscience is asserted as superior to all obligations to the State, and the State, con-

[1] This is Gibbon's translation.

fronted by this new claim, is unable to admit it. Persecution is the result.

Even from the standpoint of an orthodox and loyal pagan the persecution of the Christians is indefensible, because blood was shed uselessly. In other words, it was a great mistake because it was unsuccessful. For persecution is a choice between two evils. The alternatives are violence (which no reasonable defender of persecution would deny to be an evil in itself) and the spread of dangerous opinions. The first is chosen simply to avoid the second, on the ground that the second is the greater evil. But if the persecution is not so devised and carried out as to accomplish its end, then you have two evils instead of one, and nothing can justify this. From their point of view, the Emperors had good reasons for regarding Christianity as dangerous and anti-social, but they should either have let it alone or taken systematic measures to destroy it. If at an early stage they had established a drastic and systematic inquisition, they might possibly have exterminated it. This at least would have been statesmanlike. But they had no conception of extreme measures, and they did not understand—they had no experience to guide them—the sort of problem they had to deal with. They hoped to succeed by intimidation.

Their attempts at suppression were vacillating, fitful, and ridiculously ineffectual. The later persecutions (of A.D. 250 and 303) had no prospect of success. It is particularly to be observed that no effort was made to suppress Christian literature.

The higher problem whether persecution, even if it attains the desired end, is justifiable, was not considered. The struggle hinged on antagonism between the conscience of the individual and the authority and supposed interests of the State. It was the question which had been raised by Socrates, raised now on a wider platform in a more pressing and formidable shape: what is to happen when obedience to the law is inconsistent with obedience to an invisible master? Is it incumbent on the State to respect the conscience of the individual at all costs, or within what limits? The Christians did not attempt a solution, the general problem did not interest them. They claimed the right of freedom exclusively for themselves from a non-Christian government; and it is hardly going too far to suspect that they would have applauded the government if it had suppressed the Gnostic sects whom they hated and calumniated. In any case, when a Christian State was established, they would completely forget the principle which they had invoked. The martyrs died for conscience, but not for liberty. To-day the greatest of the Churches demands freedom of conscience in the modern States which she does not control, but refuses to admit that, where she had the power, it would be incumbent on her to concede it.

If we review the history of classical antiquity as a whole, we may almost say that freedom of thought was like the air men breathed. It was taken for granted and nobody thought about it. If seven or eight thinkers at Athens were penalized for heterodoxy, in some and perhaps in most of these cases heterodoxy was only a pretext. They do not invalidate the general facts that the advance of knowledge was not impeded by prejudice, or science retarded by the weight of unscientific authority. The educated Greeks were tolerant because they were friends of reason and did not set up any authority to overrule reason. Opinions were not imposed except by argument; you were not expected to receive some "kingdom of heaven" like a little child, or to prostrate your intellect before an authority claiming to be infallible.

But this liberty was not the result of a conscious policy or deliberate conviction, and therefore it was precarious. The problems of freedom of thought, religious liberty, toleration, had not been forced upon society and were never seriously considered. When Christianity confronted the Roman government, no one saw that in the treatment of a small, obscure, and, to pagan thinkers, uninteresting or repugnant sect, a principle of the deepest social importance was involved. A long experience of the theory and practice of persecution was required to base securely the theory of freedom of thought. The lurid policy of coercion which the Christian Church adopted, and its consequences, would at last compel reason to wrestle with the problem and discover the justification of intellectual liberty. The spirit of the Greeks and Romans, alive in their works, would, after a long period of obscuration, again enlighten the world and aid in re-establishing the reign of reason, which they had carelessly enjoyed without assuring its foundations.

CHAPTER III

REASON IN PRISON

(THE MIDDLE AGES)

About ten years after the Edict of Toleration, Constantine the Great adopted Christianity. This momentous decision inaugurated

"goes far
beyond the
facts of the
case."

a millennium in which reason was enchained, thought was enslaved, and knowledge made no progress.

During the two centuries in which they had been a forbidden sect the Christians had claimed toleration on the ground that religious belief is voluntary and not a thing which can be enforced. When their faith became the predominant creed and had the power of the State behind it, they abandoned this view. They embarked on the hopeful enterprise of bringing about a complete uniformity in men's opinions on the mysteries of the universe, and began a more or less definite policy of coercing thought. This policy was adopted by Emperors and Governments partly on political grounds; religious divisions, bitter as they were, seemed dangerous to the unity of the State. But the fundamental principle lay in the doctrine that salvation is to be found exclusively in the Christian Church. The profound conviction that those who did not believe in its doctrines would be damned eternally, and that God punishes theological error as if it were the most heinous of crimes, led naturally to persecution. It was a duty to impose on men the only true doctrine, seeing that their own eternal interests were at stake, and to hinder errors from spreading. Heretics were more than ordinary criminals and the pains that man could inflict on them were as nothing to the tortures awaiting them in hell. To rid the earth of men who, however virtuous, were, through their religious errors, enemies of the Almighty, was a plain duty. Their virtues were no excuse. We must remember that, according to the humane doctrine of the Christians, pagan, that is, merely human, virtues were vices, and infants who died unbaptized passed the rest of time in creeping on the floor of hell. The intolerance arising from such views could not but differ in kind and intensity from anything that the world had yet witnessed.

Besides the logic of its doctrines, the character of its Sacred Book must also be held partly accountable for the intolerant principles of the Christian Church. It was unfortunate that the early Christians had included in their Scripture the Jewish writings which reflect the ideas of a low stage of civilization and are full of savagery. It would be difficult to say how much harm has been done, in corrupting the morals of men, by the precepts and examples of inhumanity, violence, and bigotry which the reverent reader of the Old Testament, implicitly believing in its inspiration, is bound to approve. It furnished an armoury for the theory of

persecution. The truth is that Sacred Books
are an obstacle to moral and intellectual progress, because they consecrate the ideas of a
given epoch, and its customs, as divinely ap-
pointed. Christianity, by adopting books
of a long past age, placed in the path of
human development a particularly nasty
stumbling-block. It may occur to one to
wonder how history might have been altered
—altered it surely would have been—if the
Christians had cut Jehovah out of their
programme and, content with the New Testament, had rejected the inspiration of the
Old.

Under Constantine the Great and his successors, edict after edict fulminated against
the worship of the old pagan gods and against
heretical Christian sects. Julian the Apos-
tate, who in his brief reign (A.D. 361-3)
sought to revive the old order of things, pro-
claimed universal toleration, but he placed
Christians at a disadvantage by forbidding
them to teach in schools. This was only
a momentary check. Paganism was finally
shattered by the severe laws of Theodosius I
(end of fourth century). It lingered on here
and there for more than another century,
especially at Rome and Athens, but had little
importance. The Christians were more concerned in striving among themselves than in

crushing the prostrate spirit of antiquity. The execution of the heretic Priscillian in Spain (fourth century) inaugurated the punishment of heresy by death. It is interesting to see a non-Christian of this age teaching the Christian sects that they should suffer one another. Themistius in an address to the Emperor Valens urged him to repeal his edicts against the Christians with whom he did not agree, and expounded a theory of toleration. "The religious beliefs of individuals are a field in which the authority of a government cannot be effective; compliance can only lead to hypocritical professions. Every faith should be allowed; the civil government should govern orthodox and heterodox to the common good. God himself plainly shows that he wishes various forms of worship; there are many roads by which one can reach him."

No father of the Church has been more esteemed or enjoyed higher authority than St. Augustine (died A.D. 410). He formulated the principle of persecution for the guidance of future generations, basing it on the firm foundation of Scripture—on words used by Jesus Christ in one of his parables, "Compel them to come in." Till the end of the twelfth century the Church worked hard to suppress heterodoxies. There was much

persecution, but it was not systematic.
There is reason to think that in the pursuit
of heresy the Church was mainly guided by
considerations of its temporal interest, and
was roused to severe action only when the
spread of false doctrine threatened to reduce
its revenues or seemed a menace to society.
At the end of the twelfth century Innocent
III became Pope and under him the Church
of Western Europe reached the height of its
power. He and his immediate successors
are responsible for imagining and beginning
an organized movement to sweep heretics
out of Christendom. Languedoc in South-
western France was largely populated by heretics, whose opinions were considered particularly offensive, known as the Albigeois.
They were the subjects of the Count of
Toulouse, and were an industrious and respectable people. But the Church got far too
little money out of this anti-clerical population, and Innocent called upon the Count
to extirpate heresy from his dominion. As
he would not obey, the Pope announced a
Crusade against the Albigeois, and offered to
all who would bear a hand the usual rewards
granted to Crusaders, including absolution
from all their sins. A series of sanguinary
wars followed in which the Englishman,
Simon de Montfort, took part. There were

were even a great historian made. what a comfort to the humble.

wholesale burnings and hangings of men, women and children. The resistance of the people was broken down, though the heresy was not eradicated, and the struggle ended in 1229 with the complete humiliation of the Count of Toulouse. <u>The important point of the episode is this</u>: the Church introduced into the public law of Europe <u>the new principle that a sovran held his crown on the condition that he should extirpate heresy</u>. If he hesitated to persecute at the command of the Pope, he must be coerced; his lands were forfeited; and his dominions were thrown open to be seized by any one whom the Church could induce to attack him. The Popes thus established a theocratic system in which all other interests were to be subordinated to the grand duty of maintaining the purity of the Faith.

But in order to root out heresy it was necessary to discover it in its most secret retreats. The Albigeois had been crushed, but the poison of their doctrine was not yet destroyed. The organized system of searching out heretics known as the Inquisition was founded by Pope Gregory IX about A.D. 1233, and fully established by a Bull of Innocent IV (A.D. 1252) which regulated the machinery of persecution "as an integral part of the social edifice in every city and every

State." This powerful engine for the suppression of the freedom of men's religious opinions is unique in history.

The bishops were not equal to the new talk undertaken by the Church, and in every ecclesiastical province suitable monks were selected and to them was delegated the authority of the Pope for discovering heretics. These inquisitors had unlimited authority, they were subject to no supervision and responsible to no man. It would not have been easy to establish this system but for the fact that contemporary secular rulers had inaugurated independently a merciless legislation against heresy. The Emperor Frederick II, who was himself undoubtedly a freethinker, made laws for his extensive dominions in Italy and Germany (between 1220 and 1235), enacting that all heretics should be outlawed, that those who did not recant should be burned, those who recanted should be imprisoned, but if they relapsed should be executed; that their property should be confiscated, their houses destroyed, and their children, to the second generation, ineligible to positions of emolument unless they had betrayed their father or some other heretic.

Frederick's legislation consecrated the stake as the proper punishment for heresy. This

cruel form of death for that crime seems to
have been first inflicted on heretics by a
French king (1017). We must remember
that in the Middle Ages, and much later,
crimes of all kinds were punished with the
utmost cruelty. In England in the reign
of Henry VIII there is a case of prisoners
being boiled to death. Heresy was the foul-
est of all crimes; and to prevail against it
was to prevail against the legions of hell.
The cruel enactments against heretics were
strongly supported by the public opinion of
the masses.

When the Inquisition was fully developed
it covered Western Christendom with a net
from the meshes of which it was difficult for
a heretic to escape. The inquisitors in the
various kingdoms co-operated, and commu-
nicated information; there was "a chain of
tribunals throughout continental Europe."
England stood outside the system, but from
the age of Henry IV and Henry V the government repressed heresy by the stake under a
special statute (A.D. 1400; repealed 1533; revived under Mary; finally repealed in 1676).

In its task of imposing unity of belief the
Inquisition was most successful in Spain.
Here towards the end of the fifteenth century a system was instituted which had pecu-
liarities of its own and was very jealous of

Roman interference. One of the achievements of the Spanish Inquisition (which was not abolished till the nineteenth century) was to expel the Moriscos or converted Moors, who retained many of their old Mohammedan opinions and customs. It is also said to have eradicated Judaism and to have preserved the country from the zeal of Protestant missionaries. But it cannot be proved that it deserves the credit of having protected Spain against Protestantism, for it is quite possible that if the seeds of Protestant opinion had been sown they would, in any case, have fallen dead on an uncongenial soil. Freedom of thought however was entirely suppressed.

One of the most efficacious means for hunting down heresy was the "Edict of Faith," which enlisted the people in the service of the Inquisition and required every man to be an informer. From time to time a certain district was visited and an edict issued commanding those who knew anything of any heresy to come forward and reveal it, under fearful penalties temporal and spiritual. In consequence, no one was free from the suspicion of his neighbours or even of his own family. "No more ingenious device has been invented to subjugate a whole population, to paralyze its intellect, and to reduce it to blind obedience. It elevated delation to the rank of high religious duty."

The process employed in the trials of those accused of heresy in Spain rejected every reasonable means for the ascertainment of truth. The prisoner was assumed to be guilty, the burden of proving his innocence rested on him; his judge was virtually his prosecutor. All witnesses against him, however infamous, were admitted. The rules for allowing witnesses for the prosecution were lax; those for rejecting witnesses for the defence were rigid. Jews, Moriscos, and servants could give evidence against the prisoner but not for him, and the same rule applied to kinsmen to the fourth degree. The principle on which the Inquisition proceeded was that better a hundred innocent should suffer than one guilty person escape. Indulgences were granted to any one who contributed wood to the pile. But the tribunal of the Inquisition did not itself condemn to the stake, for the Church must not be guilty of the shedding of blood. The ecclesiastical judge pronounced the prisoner to be a heretic of whose conversion there was no hope, and handed him over ("relaxed" him was the official term) to the secular authority, asking and charging the magistrate "to treat him benignantly and mercifully." But this

formal plea for mercy could not be enter-
tained by the civil power; it had no choice
but to inflict death; if it did otherwise, it
was a promoter of heresy. All princes and
officials, according to the Canon Law, must
punish duly and promptly heretics handed
over to them by the Inquisition, under pain of
excommunication. It is to be noted that the
number of deaths at the stake has been much
over-estimated by popular imagination; but
the sum of suffering caused by the methods
of the system and the punishments that fell
short of death can hardly be exaggerated.

The legal processes employed by the
Church in these persecutions exercised a
corrupting influence on the criminal juris-
prudence of the Continent. Lea, the historian of the Inquisition, observes: "Of all
the curses which the Inquisition brought in
its train, this perhaps was the greatest—that,
until the closing years of the eighteenth century, throughout the greater part of Europe,
the inquisitorial process, as developed for the
destruction of heresy, became the customary
method of dealing with all who were under
any accusation."

The Inquisitors who, as Gibbon says,
"defended nonsense by cruelties," are often
regarded as monsters. It may be said for
them and for the kings who did their will that

they were not a bit worse than the priests and monarchs of primitive ages who sacrificed human beings to their deities. The Greek king, Agamemnon, who immolated his daughter Iphigenia to obtain favourable winds from the gods, was perhaps a most affectionate father, and the seer who advised him to do so may have been a man of high integrity. They acted according to their beliefs. And so in the Middle Ages and afterwards men of kindly temper and the purest zeal for morality were absolutely devoid of mercy where heresy was suspected. Hatred of heresy was a sort of infectious germ, generated by the doctrine of exclusive salvation.

It has been observed that this dogma also injured the sense of truth. As man's eternal fate was at stake, it seemed plainly legitimate or rather imperative to use any means to enforce the true belief—even falsehood and imposture. There was no scruple about the invention of miracles or any fictions that were edifying. A disinterested appreciation of truth will not begin to prevail till the seventeenth century.

While this principle, with the associated doctrines of sin, hell, and the last judgment, led to such consequences, there were other doctrines and implications in Christianity which, forming a solid rampart against the

advance of knowledge, blocked the paths of
science in the Middle Ages, and obstructed
its progress till the latter half of the nineteenth century. In every important field
of scientific research, the ground was occupied
by false views which the Church declared to
be true on the infallible authority of the Bible.
The Jewish account of Creation and the Fall
of Man, inextricably bound up with the
Christian theory of Redemption, excluded
from free inquiry geology, zoology, and
anthropology. The literal interpretation of
the Bible involved the truth that the sun
revolves round the earth. The Church condemned the theory of the antipodes. One
of the charges against Servetus (who was
burned in the sixteenth century; see below,
p. 79) was that he believed the statement of a
Greek geographer that Judea is a wretched
barren country in spite of the fact that the
Bible describes it as a land flowing with milk
and honey. The Greek physician Hippo-
crates had based the study of medicine and
disease on experience and methodical research. In the Middle Ages men relapsed
to the primitive notions of a barbarous age.
Bodily ailments were ascribed to occult
agencies—the malice of the Devil or the
wrath of God. St. Augustine said that the
diseases of Christians were caused by demons,

and Luther in the same way attributed them
to Satan. It was only logical that supernatural remedies should be sought to coun-
teract the effects of supernatural causes.
There was an immense traffic in relics with
miraculous virtues, and this had the advantage of bringing in a large revenue to the
Church. Physicians were often exposed to
suspicions of sorcery and unbelief. Anatomy
was forbidden, partly perhaps on account of
the doctrine of the resurrection of the body.
The opposition of ecclesiastics to inoculation
in the eighteenth century was a survival of
the mediæval view of disease. Chemistry
(alchemy) was considered a diabolical art
and in 1317 was condemned by the Pope.
The long imprisonment of Roger Bacon
(thirteenth century) who, while he professed
zeal for orthodoxy, had an inconvenient
instinct for scientific research, illustrates the
mediæval distrust of science.

It is possible that the knowledge of nature
would have progressed little, even if this
distrust of science on theological grounds had
not prevailed. For Greek science had ceased
to advance five hundred years before Christianity became powerful. After about 200
B.C. no important discoveries were made.
The explanation of this decay is not easy, but
we may be sure that it is to be sought in the

social conditions of the Greek and Roman world. And we may suspect that the social conditions of the Middle Ages would have proved unfavourable to the scientific spirit— the disinterested quest of facts—even if the controlling beliefs had not been hostile. We may suspect that the rebirth of science would in any case have been postponed till new social conditions, which began to appear in the thirteenth century (see next Chapter), had reached a certain maturity. Theological prejudice may have injured knowledge principally by its survival after the Middle Ages had passed away. In other words, the harm done by Christian doctrines, in this respect, may lie less in the obscurantism of the dark interval between ancient and modern civilization, than in the obstructions which they offered when science had revived in spite of them and could no longer be crushed.

The firm belief in witchcraft, magic, and demons was inherited by the Middle Ages from antiquity, but it became far more lurid and made the world terrible. Men believed that they were surrounded by fiends watching for every opportunity to harm them, that pestilences, storms, eclipses, and famines were the work of the Devil; but they believed as firmly that ecclesiastical rites were capable of coping with these enemies. Some of the

early Christian Emperors legislated against
magic, but till the fourteenth century there
was no systematic attempt to root out witchcraft. The fearful epidemic, known as the
Black Death, which devastated Europe in
that century, seems to have aggravated the
haunting terror of the invisible world of
demons. Trials for witchcraft multiplied,
and for three hundred years the discovery
of witchcraft and the destruction of those
who were accused of practising it, chiefly
women, was a standing feature of European
civilization. Both the theory and the persecution were supported by Holy Scripture.
"Thou shalt not suffer a witch to live" was
the clear injunction of the highest authority.
Pope Innocent VIII issued a Bull on the
matter (1484) in which he asserted that
plagues and storms are the work of witches,
and the ablest minds believed in the reality
of their devilish powers.

No story is more painful than the persecution of witches, and nowhere was it more
atrocious than in England and Scotland. I
mention it because it was the direct result
of theological doctrines, and because, as we
shall see, it was rationalism which brought
the long chapter of horrors to an end.

In the period, then, in which the Church
exercised its greatest influence, reason was

enchained in the prison which Christianity had built around the human mind. It was not indeed inactive, but its activity took the form of heresy; or, to pursue the metaphor, those who broke chains were unable for the most part to scale the walls of the prison; their freedom extended only so far as to arrive at beliefs, which, like orthodoxy itself, were based on Christian mythology. There were some exceptions to the rule. At the end of the twelfth century a stimulus from another world began to make itself felt. The philosophy of Aristotle became known to learned men in Western Christendom; their teachers were Jews and Mohammedans. Among the Mohammedans there was a certain amount of free thought, provoked by their knowledge of ancient Greek speculation. The works of the freethinker Averroes (twelfth century) which were based on Aristotle's philosophy, propagated a small wave of rationalism in Christian countries. Averroes held the eternity of matter and denied the immortality of the soul; his general view may be described as pantheism. But he sought to avoid difficulties with the orthodox authorities of Islam by laying down the doctrine of *double truth,* that is the coexistence of two independent and contradictory truths, the one philosophical, and the other religious. This did not save him from being banished from the court of the Spanish caliph. In the University of Paris his teaching produced a school of freethinkers who held that the Creation, the resurrection of the body, and other essential dogmas, might be true from the standpoint of religion but are false from the standpoint of reason. To a plain mind this seems much as if one said that the doctrine of immortality is true on Sundays but not on week-days, or that the Apostles' Creed is false in the drawing-room and true in the kitchen. This dangerous movement was crushed, and the saving principle of double truth condemned, by Pope John XXI. The spread of Averroistic and similar speculations called forth the Theology of Thomas, of Aquino in South Italy (died 1274), a most subtle thinker, whose mind had a natural turn for scepticism. He enlisted Aristotle, hitherto the guide of infidelity, on the side of orthodoxy, and constructed an ingenious Christian philosophy which is still authoritative in the Roman Church. But Aristotle and reason are dangerous allies for faith, and the treatise of Thomas is perhaps more calculated to unsettle a believing mind by the doubts which it powerfully states than to quiet the scruples of a doubter by its solutions.

There must always have been some private

and underground unbelief here and there,
which did not lead to any serious consequences. The blasphemous statement that
the world had been deceived by three im-
postors, Moses, Jesus, and Mohammed,
was current in the thirteenth century. It
was attributed to the freethinking Emperor
Frederick II (died 1250), who has been
described as "the first modern man." The
same idea, in a milder form, was expressed
in the story of the Three Rings, which is at
least as old. A Mohammedan ruler, desiring
to extort money from a rich Jew, summoned
him to his court and laid a snare for him.
"My friend," he said, "I have often heard it
reported that thou art a very wise man. Tell
me therefore which of the three religions,
that of the Jews, that of the Mohammedans,
and that of the Christians, thou believest to
be the truest." The Jew saw that a trap was
laid for him and answered as follows: "My
lord, there was once a rich man who among
his treasures had a ring of such great value
that he wished to leave it as a perpetual heir-
loom to his successors. So he made a will
that whichever of his sons should be found
in possession of this ring after his death should
be considered his heir. The son to whom he
gave the ring acted in the same way as his
father, and so the ring passed from hand to

hand. At last it came into the possession of a man who had three sons whom he loved equally. Unable to make up his mind to which of them he should leave the ring, he promised it to each of them privately, and then in order to satisfy them all caused a goldsmith to make two other rings so closely resembling the true ring that he was unable to distinguish them himself. On his death-bed he gave each of them a ring, and each claimed to be his heir, but no one could prove his title because the rings were indistinguishable, and the suit at law lasts till this day. It is even so, my lord, with the three religions, given by God to the three peoples. They each think they have the true religion, but which of them really has it, is a question, like that of the rings, still undecided." This sceptical story became famous in the eighteenth century, when the German poet, Lessing, built upon it his drama *Nathan the Sage*, which was intended to show the unreasonableness of intolerance.

CHAPTER IV

PROSPECT OF DELIVERANCE

(THE RENAISSANCE AND THE REFORMATION)

THE intellectual and social movement which was to dispel the darkness of the

Middle Ages and prepare the way for those who would ultimately deliver reason from her prison, began in Italy in the thirteenth century. The misty veil woven of credulity and infantile naïveté which had hung over men's souls and protected them from understanding either themselves or their relation to the world began to lift. The individual began to feel his separate individuality, to be conscious of his own value as a person apart from his race or country (as in the later ages of Greece and Rome); and the world around him began to emerge from the mists of mediæval dreams. The change was due to the political and social conditions of the little Italian States, of which some were republics and others governed by tyrants.

To the human world, thus unveiling itself, the individual who sought to make it serve his purposes required a guide; and the guide was found in the ancient literature of Greece and Rome. Hence the whole transformation, which presently extended from Italy to Northern Europe, is known as the *Renaissance*, or rebirth of classical antiquity. But the awakened interest in classical literature while it coloured the character and stimulated the growth of the movement, supplying new ideals and suggesting new points of view, was only the form in which the change of spirit began to express itself in the fourteenth century. The change might conceivably have taken some other shape. Its true name is Humanism.

At the time men hardly felt that they were passing into a new age of civilization, nor did the culture of the Renaissance immediately produce any open or general intellectual rebellion against orthodox beliefs. The world was gradually assuming an aspect decidedly unfriendly to the teaching of mediæval orthodoxy; but there was no explosion of hostility; it was not till the seventeenth century that war between religion and authority was systematically waged. The humanists were not hostile to theological authority or to the claims of religious dogma; but they had discovered a purely human curiosity about this world and it absorbed their interest. They idolized pagan literature which abounded in poisonous germs; the secular side of education became all-important; religion and theology were kept in a separate compartment. Some speculative minds, which were sensitive to the contradiction, might seek to reconcile the old religion with new ideas; but the general tendency of thinkers in the Renaissance period was to keep the two worlds distinct, and to practise outward conformity to the creed without any real intellectual submission.

I may illustrate this double-facedness of the Renaissance by Montaigne (second half of sixteenth century). His *Essays* make for rationalism, but contain frequent professions of orthodox Catholicism, in which he was perfectly sincere. There is no attempt to reconcile the two points of view; in fact, he takes the sceptical position that there is no bridge between reason and religion. The human intellect is incapable in the domain of theology, and religion must be placed aloft, out of reach and beyond the interference of reason; to be humbly accepted. But while he humbly accepted it, on sceptical grounds which would have induced him to accept Mohammadanism if he had been born in Cairo, his soul was not in its dominion. It was the philosophers and wise men of antiquity, Cicero, and Seneca, and Plutarch, who moulded and possessed his mind. It is to them, and not to the consolations of Christianity, that he turns when he discusses the problem of death. The religious wars in France which he witnessed and the Massacre of St. Bartholomew's Day (1572) were calculated to confirm him in his scepticism. His attitude to persecution is expressed in the remark that "it is setting a high value on one's opinions to roast men on account of them."

The logical results of Montaigne's scepticism were made visible by his friend Charron, who published a book *On Wisdom* in 1601. Here it is taught that true morality is not founded on religion, and the author surveys the history of Christianity to show the evils which it had produced. He says of immortality that it is the most generally received doctrine, the most usefully believed, and the most weakly established by human reasons; but he modified this and some other passages in a second edition. A contemporary Jesuit placed Charron in the catalogue of the most dangerous and wicked atheists. He was really a deist; but in those days, and long after, no one scrupled to call a non-Christian deist an atheist. His book would doubtless have been suppressed and he would have suffered but for the support of King Henry IV. It has a particular interest because it transports us directly from the atmosphere of the Renaissance, represented by Montaigne, into the new age of more or less aggressive rationalism.

What Humanism did in the fourteenth, fifteenth, and sixteenth centuries, at first in Italy, then in other countries, was to create an intellectual atmosphere in which the emancipation of reason could begin and knowledge could resume its progress. The period saw the invention of printing and the discovery of new parts of the globe, and these things were to aid powerfully in the future defeat of authority.

But the triumph of freedom depended on other causes also; it was not to be brought about by the intellect alone. The chief political facts of the period were the decline of the power of the Pope in Europe, the decay of the Holy Roman Empire, and the growth of strong monarchies, in which worldly interests determined and dictated ecclesiastical policy, and from which the modern State was to develop. The success of the *Reformation* was made possible by these conditions. Its victory in North Germany was due to the secular interest of the princes, who profited by the confiscation of Church lands. In England there was no popular movement; the change was carried through by the government for its own purposes.

The principal cause of the Reformation was the general corruption of the Church and the flagrancy of its oppression. For a long time the Papacy had had no higher aim than to be a secular power exploiting its spiritual authority for the purpose of promoting its worldly interests, by which it was exclusively governed. All the European States based their diplomacy on this assumption. Since the fourteenth century every one acknowledged the need of reforming the Church, and reform had been promised, but things went from bad to worse, and there was no resource but rebellion. The rebellion led by Luther was the result not of a revolt of reason against dogmas, but of widely spread anti-clerical feeling due to the ecclesiastical methods of extorting money, particularly by the sale of Indulgences, the most glaring abuse of the time. It was his study of the theory of Papal Indulgences that led Luther on to his theological heresies.

It is an elementary error, but one which is still shared by many people who have read history superficially, that the Reformation established religious liberty and the right of private judgment. What it did was to bring about a new set of political and social conditions, under which religious liberty could ultimately be secured, and, by virtue of its inherent inconsistencies, to lead to results at which its leaders would have shuddered. But nothing was further from the minds of the leading Reformers than the toleration of doctrines differing from their own. They replaced one authority by another. They set up the authority of the Bible instead of that of the Church, but it was the Bible according to Luther or the Bible according to Calvin. So far as the spirit of intolerance went, there was nothing to choose between the new and the old Churches. The religious wars were not for the cause of freedom, but for particular sets of doctrines; and in France, if the Protestants had been victorious, it is certain that they would not have given more liberal terms to the Catholics than the Catholics gave to them.

Luther was quite opposed to liberty of conscience and worship, a doctrine which was inconsistent with Scripture as he read it. He might protest against coercion and condemn the burning of heretics, when he was in fear that he and his party might be victims, but when he was safe and in power, he asserted his real view that it was the duty of the State to impose the true doctrine and exterminate heresy, which was an abomination, that unlimited obedience to their prince in religious as in other matters was the duty of subjects, and that the end of the State was to defend the faith. He held that Anabaptists should be put to the sword. With Protestants and Catholics alike the dogma of exclusive salvation led to the same place.

Calvin's fame for intolerance is blackest. He did not, like Luther, advocate the absolute power of the civil ruler; he stood for the control of the State by the Church—a form of government which is commonly called theo-

cracy; and he established a theocracy at
Geneva. Here liberty was completely
crushed; false doctrines were put down by
imprisonment, exile, and death. The punishment of Servetus is the most famous exploit
of Calvin's warfare against heresy. The
Spaniard Servetus, who had written against
the dogma of the Trinity, was imprisoned at
Lyons (partly through the machinations of
Calvin) and having escaped came rashly to
Geneva. He was tried for heresy and committed to the flames (1553), though Geneva
had no jurisdiction over him. Melanchthon,
who formulated the principles of persecution,
praised this act as a memorable example to
posterity. Posterity however was one day
to be ashamed of that example. In 1903
the Calvinists of Geneva felt impelled to
erect an expiatory monument, in which Calvin "our great Reformer" is excused as guilty
of an error "which was that of his century."

Thus the Reformers, like the Church from
which they parted, cared nothing for freedom,
they only cared for "truth." If the mediæval
ideal was to purge the world of heretics, the
object of the Protestant was to exclude all
dissidents from his own land. The people at
large were to be driven into a fold, to accept
their faith at the command of their sovran.
This was the principle laid down in the

religious peace which (1555) composed the
struggle between the Catholic Emperor and
the Protestant German princes. It was
recognized by Catherine de' Medici when
she massacred the French Protestants and
signified to Queen Elizabeth that *she* might
do likewise with English Catholics.

Nor did the Protestant creeds represent
enlightenment. The Reformation on the
Continent was as hostile to enlightenment as
it was to liberty; and science, if it seemed
to contradict the Bible, has as little chance
with Luther as with the Pope. The Bible,
interpreted by the Protestants or the Roman
Church, was equally fatal to witches. In
Germany the development of learning received a long set-back.

Yet the Reformation involuntarily helped
the cause of liberty. The result was contrary
to the intentions of its leaders, was indirect,
and long delayed. In the first place, the
great rent in Western Christianity, substi-
tuting a number of theological authorities
instead of one—several gods, we may say,
instead of one God—produced a weakening
of ecclesiastical authority in general. The
religious tradition was broken. In the second
place, in the Protestant States, the supreme
ecclesiastical power was vested in the sovran;
the sovran had other interests besides those of

the Church to consider; and political reasons
would compel him sooner or later to modify
the principle of ecclesiastical intolerance.
Catholic States in the same way were forced
to depart from the duty of not suffering heretics. The religious wars in France ended in a
limited toleration of Protestants. The policy
of Cardinal Richelieu, who supported the
Protestant cause in Germany, illustrates how
secular interests obstructed the cause of faith.

Again, the intellectual justification of the
Protestant rebellion against the Church had
been the right of private judgment, that is,
the principle of religious liberty. But the
Reformers had asserted it only for themselves, and as soon as they had framed their
own articles of faith, they had practically
repudiated it. This was the most glaring
inconsistency in the Protestant position; and
the claim which they had thrust aside could
not be permanently suppressed. Once more,
the Protestant doctrines rested on an insecure
foundation which no logic could defend, and
inevitably led from one untenable position to
another. If we are to believe on authority,
why should we prefer the upstart dictation of
the Lutheran Confession of Augsburg or the
English Thirty-nine Articles to the venerable
authority of the Church of Rome? If we
decide against Rome, we must do so by means

of reason; but once we exercise reason in the matter, why should we stop where Luther or Calvin or any of the other rebels stopped, unless we assume that one of them was inspired? If we reject superstitions which they rejected, there is nothing except *their* authority to prevent us from rejecting all or some of the superstitions which they retained. Moreover, their Bible-worship promoted results which they did not foresee.[1] The inspired record on which the creeds depend became an open book. Public attention was directed to it as never before, though it cannot be said to have been universally read before the nineteenth century. Study led to criticism, the difficulties of the dogma of inspiration were appreciated, and the Bible was ultimately to be submitted to a remorseless dissection which has altered at least the quality of its authority in the eyes of intelligent believers. This process of Biblical criticism has been conducted mainly in a Protestant atmosphere and the new position in which the Bible was placed by the Reformation must be held partly accountable. In these ways, Protestantism was adapted to be a stepping-stone to rationalism, and thus served the cause of freedom.

[1] The danger, however, was felt in Germany, and in the seventeenth century the study of Scripture was not encouraged at German Universities.

That cause however was powerfully and directly promoted by one sect of Reformers, who in the eyes of all the others were blasphemers and of whom most people never think when they talk of the Reformation. I mean the Socinians. Of their far-reaching influence something will be said in the next chapter.

Another result of the Reformation has still to be mentioned, its renovating effect on the Roman Church, which had now to fight for its existence. A new series of Popes who were in earnest about religion began with Paul III (1534) and reorganized the Papacy and its resources for a struggle of centuries.[1] The institution of the Jesuit order, the establishment of the Inquisition at Rome, the Council of Trent, the censorship of the Press (Index of Forbidden Books) were the expression of the new spirit and the means to cope with the new situation. The reformed Papacy was good fortune for believing children of the Church, but what here concerns us is that one of its chief objects was to repress freedom more effectually. Savonarola who preached right living at Florence had been executed (1498) under Pope Alexander VI who was a notorious profligate. If Savonarola had lived

[1] See Barry, *Papacy and Modern Times* (in this series), 113 *seq.*

in the new era he might have been canonized,
but Giordano Bruno was burned.

Giordano Bruno had constructed a religious
philosophy, based partly upon Epicurus,
from whom he took the theory of the infinity
of the universe. But Epicurean materialism
was transformed into a pantheistic mysticism
by the doctrine that God is the soul of matter. Accepting the recent discovery of Copernicus, which Catholics and Protestants
alike rejected, that the earth revolves round
the sun, Bruno took the further step of regarding the fixed stars as suns, each with its invisible satellites. He sought to come to an
understanding with the Bible, which (he held)
being intended for the vulgar had to accom-
modate itself to their prejudices. Leaving
Italy, because he was suspected of heresy, he
lived successively in Switzerland, France, England, and Germany, and in 1592, induced by a
false friend to return to Venice he was seized
by order of the Inquisition. Finally condemned in Rome, he was burned (1600) in
the Campo de' Fiori, where a monument now
stands in his honour, erected some years ago,
to the great chagrin of the Roman Church.

Much is made of the fate of Bruno because
he is one of the world's famous men. No
country has so illustrious a victim of that era
to commemorate as Italy, but in other lands

blood just as innocent was shed for heterodox
opinions. In France there was rather more
freedom than elsewhere under the relatively
tolerant government of Henry IV and of the
Cardinals Richelieu and Mazarin, till about
1660. But at Toulouse (1619) Lucilio Vanini,
a learned Italian who like Bruno wandered
about Europe, was convicted as an atheist
and blasphemer; his tongue was torn out
and he was burned. Protestant England,
under Elizabeth and James I, did not lag
behind the Roman Inquisition, but on account of the obscurity of the victims her zeal
for faith has been unduly forgotten. Yet,
but for an accident, she might have covered
herself with the glory of having done to death
a heretic not less famous than Giordano
Bruno. The poet Marlowe was accused of
atheism, but while the prosecution was hang-
ing over him he was killed in a sordid quarrel in a tavern (1593). Another dramatist
(Kyd) who was implicated in the charge was
put to the torture. At the same time Sir
Walter Raleigh was prosecuted for unbelief
but not convicted. Others were not so fortu-
nate. Three or four persons were burned
at Norwich in the reign of Elizabeth for un-
christian doctrines, among them Francis
Kett who had been a Fellow of Corpus
Christi, Cambridge. Under James I, who

interested himself personally in such matters,
Bartholomew Legate was charged with holding various pestilent opinions. The king
summoned him to his presence and asked him
whether he did not pray daily to Jesus Christ.
Legate replied he had prayed to Christ in the
days of his ignorance, but not for the last
seven years. "Away, base fellow," said
James, spurning him with his foot, "it shall
never be said that one stayeth in my palace
that hath never prayed to our Saviour for
seven years together." Legate, having been
imprisoned for some time in Newgate, was
declared an incorrigible heretic and burned
at Smithfield (1611). Just a month later,
one Wightman was burned at Lichfield, by
the Bishop of Coventry, for heterodox doctrines. It is possible that public opinion
was shocked by these two burnings. They
were the last cases in England of death for
unbelief. Puritan intolerance, indeed, passed
an ordinance in 1648, by which all who denied
the Trinity, Christ's divinity, the inspiration
of Scripture, or a future state, were liable to
death, and persons guilty of other heresies,
to imprisonment. But this did not lead to
any executions.

The Renaissance age saw the first signs of
the beginning of modern science, but the
mediæval prejudices against the investiga-

tion of nature were not dissipated till the seventeenth century, and in Italy they continued to a much later period. The history of modern astronomy begins in 1543, with the publication of the work of Copernicus revealing the truth about the motions of the earth. The appearance of this work is important in the history of free thought, because it raised a clear and definite issue between science and Scripture; and Osiander, who edited it (Copernicus was dying), foreseeing the outcry it would raise, stated untruly in the preface that the earth's motion was put forward only as a hypothesis. The theory was denounced by Catholics and Reformers, and it did not convince some men (*e.g.* Bacon) who were not influenced by theological prejudice. The observations of the Italian astronomer Galileo de' Galilei demonstrated the Copernican theory beyond question. His telescope discovered the moons of Jupiter, and his observation of the spots in the sun confirmed the earth's rotation. In the pulpits of Florence, where he lived under the protection of the Grand Duke, his sensational discoveries were condemned. "Men of *Galilee*, why stand ye gazing up into heaven?" He was then denounced to the Holy Office of the Inquisition by two Dominican monks. Learning that his investigations were being considered at Rome, Galileo went thither, confident that he would be able to convince the ecclesiastical authorities of the manifest truth of Copernicanism. He did not realize what theology was capable of. In February 1616 the Holy Office decided that the Copernican system was in itself absurd, and, in respect of Scripture, heretical. Cardinal Bellarmin, by the Pope's direction, summoned Galileo and officially admonished him to abandon his opinion and cease to teach it, otherwise the Inquisition would proceed against him. Galileo promised to obey. The book of Copernicus was placed on the Index. It has been remarked that Galileo's book on *Solar Spots* contains no mention of Scripture, and thus the Holy Office, in its decree which related to that book, passed judgment on a scientific, not a theological, question.

Galileo was silenced for a while, but it was impossible for him to be mute for ever. Under a new Pope (Urban VIII) he looked for greater liberty, and there were many in the Papal circle who were well disposed to him. He hoped to avoid difficulties by the device of placing the arguments for the old and the new theories side by side, and pretending not to judge between them. He wrote a treatise on the two systems (the Ptolemaic and the Copernican) in the form

of *Dialogues*, of which the preface declares
that the purpose is to explain the pros and
cons of the two views.   But the spirit of the
work is Copernican.   He received permission,
quite definite as he thought, from Father
Riccardi (master of the Sacred Palace) to
print it, and it appeared in 1632.   The Pope
however disapproved of it, the book was examined by a commission, and Galileo was
summoned before the Inquisition.   He was
old and ill, and the humiliations which
he had to endure are a painful story.   He
would probably have been more severely
treated, if one of the members of the tribunal
had not been a man of scientific training
(Macolano, a Dominican), who was able to
appreciate his ability.   Under examination,
Galileo denied that he had upheld the motion of the earth in the *Dialogues*, and asserted that he had shown the reasons of
Copernicus to be inconclusive.   This defence was in accordance with the statement
in his preface, but contradicted his deepest
conviction.   In struggling with such a tribunal, it was the only line which a man who
was not a hero could take.   At a later
session, he forced himself ignominiously
to confess that some of the arguments on the
Copernican side had been put too strongly
and to declare himself ready to confute the

theory. In the final examination, he was threatened with torture. He said that before the decree of 1616 he had held the truth of the Copernican system to be arguable, but since then he had held the Ptolemaic to be true. Next day, he publicly abjured the scientific truth which he had demonstrated. He was allowed to retire to the country, on condition that he saw no one. In the last months of his life he wrote to a friend to this effect: "The falsity of the Copernican system cannot be doubted, especially by us Catholics. It is refuted by the irrefragable authority of Scripture. The conjectures of Copernicus and his disciples were all disposed of by the one solid argument: God's omnipotence can operate in infinitely various ways. If something appears to our observation to happen in one particular way, we must not curtail God's arm, and sustain a thing in which we may be deceived." The irony is evident.

Rome did not permit the truth about the solar system to be taught till after the middle of the eighteenth century, and Galileo's books remained on the Index till 1835. The prohibition was fatal to the study of natural science in Italy.

The Roman Index reminds us of the significance of the invention of printing in the struggle for freedom of thought, by mak-

ing it easy to propagate new ideas far and
wide. Authority speedily realized the danger, and took measures to place its yoke on
the new contrivance, which promised to
be such a powerful ally of reason. Pope
Alexander VI inaugurated censorship of the
Press by his Bull against unlicensed printing
(1501). In France King Henry II made
printing without official permission punishable
by death. In Germany, censorship was introduced in 1529. In England, under Elizabeth,
books could not be printed without a license,
and printing presses were not allowed except
in London, Oxford, and Cambridge; the regu-
lation of the Press was under the authority
of the Star Chamber. Nowhere did the Press
become really free till the nineteenth century.

While the Reformation and the renovated
Roman Church meant a reaction against the
Renaissance, the vital changes which the
Renaissance signified—individualism, a new
intellectual attitude to the world, the cultivation of secular knowledge—were permanent
and destined to lead, amid the competing
intolerances of Catholic and Protestant
powers, to the goal of liberty. We shall see
how reason and the growth of knowledge
undermined the bases of theological authority. At each step in this process, in
which philosophical speculation, historical

criticism, natural science have all taken part, the opposition between reason and faith deepened; doubt, clear or vague, increased; and secularism, derived from the Humanists, and always implying scepticism, whether latent or conscious, substituted an interest in the fortunes of the human race upon earth for the interest in a future world. And along with this steady intellectual advance, toleration gained ground and freedom won more champions. In the meantime the force of political circumstances was compelling governments to mitigate their maintenance of one religious creed by measures of relief to other Christian sects, and the principle of exclusiveness was broken down for reasons of worldly expediency. *Religious* liberty was an important step towards complete freedom of opinion.

CHAPTER V

RELIGIOUS TOLERATION

In the third century B.C. the Indian king Asoka, a man of religious zeal but of tolerant spirit, confronted by the struggle between two hostile religions (Brahmanism and Buddhism), decided that both should be equally privileged and honoured in his dominions. His ordinances on the matter are memorable as the earliest existing Edicts of toleration. In Europe, as we saw, the principle of toleration was for the first time definitely expressed in the Roman Imperial Edicts which terminated the persecution of the Christians.

The religious strife of the sixteenth century raised the question in its modern form, and for many generations it was one of the chief problems of statesmen and the subject of endless controversial pamphlets. Toleration means incomplete religious liberty, and there are many degrees of it. It might be granted to certain Christian sects; it might be granted to Christian sects, but these alone; it might be granted to all religions, but not to freethinkers; or to deists, but not to atheists. It might mean the concession of some civil rights, but not of others; it might mean the exclusion of those who are tolerated from public offices or from certain professions. The religious liberty now enjoyed in Western lands has been gained through various stages of toleration.

We owe the modern principle of toleration to the Italian group of Reformers, who rejected the doctrine of the Trinity and were the fathers of Unitarianism. The Reformation movement had spread to Italy, but Rome was successful in suppressing it, and many heretics fled to Switzerland. The anti-Trini-

tarian group were forced by the intolerance of Calvin to flee to Transylvania and
Poland where they propagated their doctrines. The Unitarian creed was moulded
by Fausto Sozzini, generally known as
Socinus, and in the catechism of his sect
(1574) persecution is condemned. This re-
pudiation of the use of force in the interest of
religion is a consequence of the Socinian doctrines. For, unlike Luther and Calvin, the
Socinians conceded such a wide room to individual judgment in the interpretation of
Scripture that to impose Socinianism would
have been inconsistent with its principles.
In other words, there was a strong rationalistic element which was lacking in the Trini-
tarian creeds.

It was under the influence of the Socinian
spirit that Castellion of Savoy sounded the
trumpet of toleration in a pamphlet denouncing the burning of Servetus, whereby he
earned the malignant hatred of Calvin. He
maintained the innocence of error and ridi-
culed the importance which the Churches
laid on obscure questions such as predesti-
nation and the Trinity. "To discuss the difference between the Law and the Gospel,
gratuitous remission of sins or imputed righteousness, is as if a man were to discuss
whether a prince was to come on horseback,

or in a chariot, or dressed in white or in red." [1]
Religion is a curse if persecution is a necessary part of it.

For a long time the Socinians and those
who came under their influence when, driven
from Poland, they passed into Germany and
Holland, were the only sects which advocated
toleration.   It was adopted from them by the
Anabaptists and by the Arminian section of
the Reformed Church of Holland.   And in
Holland, the founder of the English Congregationalists, who (under the name of Independents) played such an important part in the history of the Civil War and the Commonwealth,
learned the principle of liberty of conscience.

Socinus thought that this principle could
be realized without abolishing the State
Church.   He contemplated a close union
between the State and the prevailing Church,
combined with complete toleration for other
sects.   It is under this system (which has
been called *jurisdictional*) that religious liberty has been realized in European States.
But there is another and simpler method, that
of *separating* Church from State and placing
all religions on an equality.   This was the
solution which the Anabaptists would have
preferred.   They detested the State; and
the doctrine of religious liberty was not

[1] Translated by Lecky.

precious to them.   Their ideal system would
have been an Anabaptist theocracy; separation was the second best.

In Europe, public opinion was not ripe for
separation, inasmuch as the most powerful
religious bodies were alike in regarding toleration as wicked indifference.   But it was
introduced in a small corner of the new world
beyond the Atlantic in the seventeenth
century. The Puritans who fled from the
intolerance of the English Church and State
and founded colonies in New England, were
themselves equally intolerant, not only to
Anglicans and Catholics, but to Baptists and
Quakers. They set up theocratical governments from which all who did not belong to
their own sect were excluded. Roger Williams had imbibed from the Dutch Arminians
the idea of separation of Church from State.
On account of this heresy he was driven
from Massachusetts, and he founded Providence to be a refuge for those whom the Puritan colonists persecuted. Here he set up a
democratic constitution in which the magistrates had power only in civil matters and
could not interfere with religion. Other
towns were presently founded in Rhode
Island, and a charter of Charles II (1663)
confirmed the constitution, which secured to
all citizens professing Christianity, of what-

ever form, the full enjoyment of political rights. Non-Christians were tolerated, but were not admitted to the political rights of Christians. So far, the new State fell short of perfect liberty. But the fact that Jews were soon admitted, notwithstanding, to full citizenship shows how free the atmosphere was. To Roger Williams belongs the glory of having founded the first modern State which was really tolerant and was based on the principle of taking the control of religious matters entirely out of the hands of the civil government.

Toleration was also established in the Roman Catholic colony of Maryland, but in a different way. Through the influence of Lord Baltimore an Act of Toleration was passed in 1649, notable as the first decree, voted by a legal assembly, granting complete freedom to all Christians. No one professing faith in Christ was to be molested in regard to his religion. But the law was heavy on all outside this pale. Any one who blasphemed God or attacked the Trinity or any member of the Trinity was threatened by the penalty of death. The tolerance of Maryland attracted so many Protestant settlers from Virginia that the Protestants became a majority, and as soon as they won political preponderance, they introduced an Act (1654) excluding Papists and Prelatists from toleration. The rule of the Baltimores was restored after 1660, and the old religious freedom was revived, but with the accession of William III the Protestants again came into power and the toleration which the Catholics had instituted in Maryland came to an end.

It will be observed that in both these cases freedom was incomplete; but it was much larger and more fundamental in Rhode Island, where it had been ultimately derived from the doctrine of Socinus.[1] When the colonies became independent of England the Federal Constitution which they set up was absolutely secular, but it was left to each member of the Union to adopt Separation or not (1789). If separation has become the rule in the American States, it may be largely due to the fact that on any other system the governments would have found it difficult to impose mutual tolerance on the sects. It must be added that in Maryland and a few southern States atheists still suffer from some political disabilities.

In England, the experiment of Separation would have been tried under the Commonwealth, if the Independents had had their way. This policy was overruled by Crom-

---

[1] Complete toleration was established by Penn in the Quaker Colony of Pennsylvania in 1682.

well. The new national Church included Presbyterians, Independents, and Baptists, but liberty of worship was granted to all Christian sects, except Roman Catholics and Anglicans. If the parliament had had the power, this toleration would have been a mere name. The Presbyterians regarded toleration as a work of the Devil, and would have persecuted the Independents if they could. But under Cromwell's autocratic rule even the Anglicans lived in peace, and toleration was extended to the Jews. In these days, voices were raised from various quarters advocating toleration on general grounds.[1] The most illustrious advocate was Milton, the poet, who was in favour of the severance of Church from State.

In Milton's *Areopagitica: a speech for the liberty of unlicensed printing* (1644), the freedom of the Press is eloquently sustained by arguments which are valid for freedom of thought in general. It is shown that the censorship will conduce "to the discouragement of all learning and the stop of truth, not only by disexercising and blunting our abilities in what we know already, but by hindering and cropping the discovery that might be yet further made, both in religious

---

[1] Especially Chillingworth's *Religion of Protestants* (1637), and Jeremy Taylor's *Liberty of Prophesying* (1646).

and civil wisdom." For knowledge is advanced through the utterance of new opinions, and truth is discovered by free discussion. If the waters of truth "flow not in a perpetual progression they sicken into a muddy pool of conformity and tradition." Books which are authorized by the licensers are apt to be, as Bacon said, "but the language of the times," and do not contribute to progress. The examples of the countries where the censorship is severe do not suggest that it is useful for morals: "look into Italy and Spain, whether those places be one scruple the better, the honester, the wiser, the chaster, since all the inquisitional rigour that hath been executed upon books." Spain indeed could reply, "We are, what is more important, more orthodox." It is interesting to notice that Milton places freedom of thought above civil liberty: "Give me the liberty to know, to utter, and to argue freely according to conscience, above all other liberties."

With the restoration of the Monarchy and the Anglican Church, religious liberty was extinguished by a series of laws against Dissenters. To the Revolution we owe the Act of Toleration (1689) from which the religious freedom which England enjoys at present is derived. It granted freedom of worship to Presbyterians, Congregationalists,

Baptists and Quakers, but only to these;
Catholics and Unitarians were expressly
excepted and the repressive legislation of
Charles II remained in force against them.
It was a characteristically English measure,
logically inconsistent and absurd, a mixture
of tolerance and intolerance, but suitable to
the circumstances and the state of public
opinion at the time.

In the same year John Locke's famous
(first) *Letter concerning Toleration* appeared
in Latin. Three subsequent letters developed and illustrated his thesis. The main
argument is based on the principle that
the business of civil government is quite
distinct from that of religion, that the State
is a society constituted only for preserving
and promoting the civil interests of its members—civil interests meaning life, liberty,
health, and the possession of property. The
care of souls is not committed to magistrates
more than to other men. For the magistrate
can only use outward force; but true religion
means the inward persuasion of the mind, and
the mind is so made that force cannot compel
it to believe. So too it is absurd for a State
to make laws to enforce a religion, for laws are
useless without penalties, and penalties are
impertinent because they cannot convince.

Moreover, even if penalties could change

men's beliefs, this would not conduce to the
salvation of souls. Would more men be
saved if all blindly resigned themselves to the
will of their rulers and accepted the religion
of their country? For as the princes of the
world are divided in religion, one country
alone would be in the right, and all the rest
of the world would have to follow *their* princes
to destruction; "and that which heightens
the absurdity, and very ill suits the notion of
a deity, men would owe their eternal happiness or their eternal misery to the places
of their nativity." This is a principle on
which Locke repeatedly insists. If a State
is justified in imposing a creed, it follows
that in all the lands, except the one or few
in which the true faith prevails, it is the
duty of the subjects to embrace a false religion. If Protestantism is promoted in
England, Popery by the same rule will be
promoted in France. "What is true and
good in England will be true and good at
Rome too, in China, or Geneva." Toleration is the principle which gives to the true
faith the best chance of prevailing.

Locke would concede full liberty to idol-
aters, by whom he means the Indians of
North America, and he makes some scathing
remarks on the ecclesiastical zeal which
forced these "innocent pagans" to forsake

their ancient religion. But his toleration, though it extends beyond the Christian pale, is not complete. He excepts in the first place Roman Catholics, not on account of their theological dogmas but because they "teach that faith is not to be kept with heretics," that "kings excommunicated forfeit their crowns and kingdoms," and because they deliver themselves up to the protection and service of a foreign prince—the Pope. In other words, they are politically dangerous. His other exception is atheists. "Those are not all to be tolerated who deny the being of God. Promises, covenants and oaths, which are the bonds of human society, can have no hold upon an atheist. The taking away of God, though but even in thought, dissolves all. Besides also, those that by their atheism undermine and destroy all religion, can have no pretence of religion to challenge the privilege of a Toleration."

Thus Locke is not free from the prejudices of his time. These exceptions contradict his own principle that "it is absurd that things should be enjoined by laws which are not in men's power to perform. And to believe this or that to be true does not depend upon our will." This applies to Roman Catholics as to Protestants, to atheists as to deists. Locke, however, perhaps thought that the speculative opinion of atheism, which was uncommon in his day, does depend on the will. He would have excluded from his State his great contemporary Spinoza.

But in spite of its limitations Locke's *Toleration* is a work of the highest value, and its argument takes us further than its author went. It asserts unrestrictedly the secular principle, and its logical issue is Disestablishment. A Church is merely "a free and voluntary society." I may notice the remark that if infidels were to be converted by force, it was easier for God to do it "with armies of heavenly legions than for any son of the Church, how potent soever, with all his dragoons." This is a polite way of stating a maxim analogous to that of the Emperor Tiberius (above, p. 41). If false beliefs are an offence to God, it is, really, his affair.

The toleration of Nonconformists was far from pleasing extreme Anglicans, and the influence of this party at the beginning of the eighteenth century menaced the liberty of Dissenters. The situation provoked Defoe, who was a zealous Nonconformist, to write his pamphlet, *The Shortest Way with the Dissenters* (1702), an ironical attack upon the principle of toleration. It pretends to show that the Dissenters are at heart incorrigible rebels, that a gentle policy is useless, and sug-

gests that all preachers at conventicles should
be hanged and all persons found attending such
meetings should be banished. This exceedingly amusing but terribly earnest caricature
of the sentiments of the High Anglican party
at first deceived and alarmed the Dissenters
themselves. But the High Churchmen were
furious. Defoe was fined, exposed in the pillory three times, and sent to Newgate prison.

But the Tory reaction was only temporary.
During the eighteenth century a relatively
tolerant spirit prevailed among the Christian
sects and new sects were founded. The
official Church became less fanatical; many
of its leading divines were influenced by
rationalistic thought. If it had not been
for the opposition of King George III, the
Catholics might have been freed from their
disabilities before the end of the century.
This measure, eloquently advocated by Burke
and desired by Pitt, was not carried till 1829,
and then under the threat of a revolution in
Ireland. In the meantime legal toleration had
been extended to the Unitarians in 1813, but
they were not relieved from all disabilities till
the forties. Jews were not admitted to the
full rights of citizenship till 1858.

The achievement of religious liberty in
England in the nineteenth century has been
mainly the work of Liberals. The Liberal

party has been moving towards the ultimate
goal of complete secularization and the separation of the Church from the State—
the logical results of Locke's theory of civil
government. The Disestablishment of the
Church in Ireland in 1869 partly realized this
ideal, and now more than forty years later
the Liberal party is seeking to apply the
principle to Wales. It is highly characteristic of English politics and English psychology
that the change should be carried out in this
piecemeal fashion. In the other countries of
the British Empire the system of Separation
prevails; there is no connection between the
State and any sect; no Church is anything
more than a voluntary society. But secularization has advanced under the State
Church system. It is enough to mention the
Education Act of 1870 and the abolition of
religious tests at Universities (1871). Other
gains for freedom will be noticed when I
come to speak in another chapter of the
progress of rationalism.

If we compare the religious situation in
France in the seventeenth with that in the
eighteenth century, it seems to be sharply
contrasted with the development in England.
In England there was a great advance towards religious liberty, in France there was a
falling away. Until 1676 the French Protes-

tants (Huguenots) were tolerated; for the next hundred years they were outlaws. But the toleration, which their charter (the Edict of Nantes, 1598) secured them, was of a limited kind. They were excluded, for instance, from the army; they were excluded from Paris and other cities and districts. And the liberty which they enjoyed was confined to them; it was not granted to any other sect. The charter was faithfully maintained by the two great Cardinals (Richelieu and Mazarin) who governed France under Louis XIII and Louis XIV, but when the latter assumed the active power in 1661 he began a series of laws against the Protestants which culminated in the revoking of the charter (1676) and the beginning of a Protestant persecution.

The French clergy justified this policy by the notorious text "Compel them to come in," and appealed to St. Augustine. Their arguments evoked a defence of toleration by Bayle, a French Protestant who had taken refuge in Holland. It was entitled a *Philosophical Commentary on the text "Compel them to come in"* (1686) and in importance stands beside Locke's work which was being composed at the same time. Many of the arguments urged by the two writers are identical. They agreed, and for the same reasons, in excluding Roman Catholics. The

most characteristic thing in Bayle's treatise is
his sceptical argument that, even if it were a
right principle to suppress error by force, no
truth is certain enough to justify us in applying
the theory.   We shall see (next chapter) this
eminent scholar's contribution to rationalism.

Though there was an immense exodus of
Protestants from France, Louis did not succeed in his design of extirpating heresy from
his lands.   In the eighteenth century, under
Louis XV, the presence of Protestants was
tolerated though they were outlaws; their
marriages were not recognized as legal, and
they were liable at any moment to persecution.   About the middle of the century a
literary agitation began, conducted mainly
by rationalists, but finally supported by
enlightened Catholics, to relieve the affliction
of the oppressed sect.   It resulted at last in
an Edict of Toleration (1787), which made the
position of the Protestants endurable, though
it excluded them from certain careers.

The most energetic and forceful leader in
the campaign against intolerance was Voltaire (see next chapter), and his exposure of
some glaring cases of unjust persecution did
more than general arguments to achieve the
object.   The most infamous case was that of
Jean Calas, a Protestant merchant of Toulouse, whose son committed suicide.   A report

was set abroad that the young man had decided to join the Catholic Church, and that his father, mother, and brother, filled with Protestant bigotry, killed him, with the help of a friend. They were all put in irons, tried, and condemned, though there were no arguments for their guilt, except the conjecture of bigotry. Jean Calas was broken on the wheel, his son and daughter cast into convents, his wife left to starve. Through the activity of Voltaire, then living near Geneva, the widow was induced to go to Paris, where she was kindly received, and assisted by eminent lawyers; a judicial inquiry was made; the Toulouse sentence was reversed and the King granted pensions to those who had suffered. This scandal could only have happened in the provinces, according to Voltaire: "at Paris," he says, "fanaticism, powerful though it may be, is always controlled by reason."

The case of Sirven, though it did not end tragically, was similar, and the government of Toulouse was again responsible. He was accused of having drowned his daughter in a well to hinder her from becoming a Catholic, and was, with his wife, sentenced to death. Fortunately he and his family had escaped to Switzerland, where they persuaded Voltaire of their innocence. To get the sentence reversed was the work of nine years, and this

time it was reversed at Toulouse. When
Voltaire visited Paris in 1778 he was ac-
claimed by crowds as the "defender of Calas
and the Sirvens." His disinterested practical activity against persecution was of far
more value than the treatise on *Toleration*
which he wrote in connexion with the Calas
episode. It is a poor work compared with
those of Locke and Bayle. The tolerance
which he advocates is of a limited kind; he
would confine public offices and dignities to
those who belong to the State religion.

But if Voltaire's system of toleration is
limited, it is wide compared with the religious
establishment advocated by his contemporary, Rousseau. Though of Swiss birth,
Rousseau belongs to the literature and
history of France; but it was not for nothing that he was brought up in the traditions
of Calvinistic Geneva. His ideal State
would, in its way, have been little better
than any theocracy. He proposed to establish a "civil religion" which was to be a sort
of undogmatic Christianity. But certain
dogmas, which he considered essential, were
to be imposed on all citizens on pain of
banishment. Such were the existence of a
deity, the future bliss of the good and punishment of the bad, the duty of tolerance
towards all those who accepted the funda-

mental articles of faith.   It may be said that
a State founded on this basis would be fairly
inclusive—that all Christian sects| and many
deists could find a place in it.   But by imposing indispensable beliefs, it denies the principle
of toleration.   The importance of Rousseau's
idea lies in the fact that it inspired one of
the experiments in religious policy which were
made during the French Revolution

The Revolution established religious liberty
in France. Most of the leaders were unorthodox.   Their rationalism was naturally
of the eighteenth-century type, and in the
preamble to the Declaration of Rights (1789)
deism was asserted by the words "in the
presence and under the auspices of the Supreme Being" (against which only one voice
protested).   The Declaration laid down that
no one was to be vexed on account of his
religious opinions provided he did not thereby
trouble public order.   Catholicism was retained as the "dominant" religion; Protestants (but not Jews) were admitted to
public office.   Mirabeau, the greatest statesman of the day, protested strongly against
the use of words like "tolerance" and "dominant."   He said: "The most unlimited
liberty of religion is in my eyes a right so
sacred that to express it by the word 'toleration' seems to me itself a sort of tyranny,

since the authority which tolerates might
also not tolerate." The same protest was
made in Thomas Paine's *Rights of Man* which
appeared two years later: "Toleration is not
the *opposite* of Intolerance, but is the *counter-
feit* of it. Both are despotisms. The one
assumes itself the right of withholding liberty
of conscience, and the other of granting it."
Paine was an ardent deist, and he added:
"Were a bill brought into any parliament, entitled 'An Act to tolerate or grant liberty to
the Almighty to receive the worship of a Jew
or a Turk,' or 'to prohibit the Almighty from
receiving it,' all men would startle and call
it blasphemy. There would be an uproar.
The presumption of toleration in religious
matters would then present itself unmasked."

The Revolution began well, but the spirit
of Mirabeau was not in the ascendant
throughout its course. The vicissitudes in
religious policy from 1789 to 1801 have a
particular interest, because they show that
the principle of liberty of conscience was far
from possessing the minds of the men who
were proud of abolishing the intolerance of
the government which they had overthrown.
The State Church was reorganized by the
Civil Constitution of the Clergy (1790), by
which French citizens were forbidden to
acknowledge the authority of the Pope and

the appointment of Bishops was trans-
ferred to the Electors of the Departments, so
that the commanding influence passed from
the Crown to the nation. Doctrine and
worship were not touched. Under the democratic Republic which succeeded the fall of
the monarchy (1792–5) this Constitution
was maintained, but a movement to dechris-
tianize France was inaugurated, and the
Commune of Paris ordered the churches of
all religions to be closed. The worship of
Reason, with rites modelled on the Catholic,
was organized in Paris and the provinces.
The government, violently anti-Catholic,
did not care to use force against the prevalent faith; direct persecution would have
weakened the national defence and scandal-
ized Europe. They naïvely hoped that the
superstition would disappear by degrees.
Robespierre declared against the policy of
unchristianizing France, and when he had
the power (April, 1795), he established as a
State religion the worship of the Supreme
Being. "The French people recognizes the
existence of the Supreme Being and the immortality of the Soul"; the liberty of other
cults was maintained. Thus, for a few
months, Rousseau's idea was more or less
realized. It meant intolerance. Atheism
was regarded as a vice, and "all were atheists who did not think like Robespierre."

The democratic was succeeded by the middle-class Republic (1795–9), and the policy of its government was to hinder the preponderance of any one religious group; to hold the balance among all the creeds, but with a certain partiality against the strongest, the Catholic, which threatened, as was thought, to destroy the others or even the Republic. The plan was to favour the growth of new rationalistic cults, and to undermine revealed religion by a secular system of education. Accordingly the Church was separated from the State by the Constitution of 1795, which affirmed the liberty of all worship and withdrew from the Catholic clergy the salaries which the State had hitherto paid. The elementary schools were laicized. The Declaration of Rights, the articles of the Constitution, and republican morality were taught instead of religion. An enthusiast declared that "the religion of Socrates, Marcus Aurelius, and Cicero would soon be the religion of the world."

A new rationalistic religion was introduced under the name of Theophilanthropy. It was the "natural religion" of the philosophers and poets of the century, of Voltaire and the English deists—not the purified Christianity of Rousseau, but anterior and superior to Christianity. Its doctrines, briefly formulated, were: God, immortality, fraternity, humanity; no attacks on other religions, but respect and honour towards all; gatherings in a family, or in a temple, to encourage one another to practise morality. Protected by the government sometimes secretly, sometimes openly, it had a certain success among the cultivated classes.

The idea of the lay State was popularized under this rule, and by the end of the century there was virtually religious peace in France. Under the Consulate (from 1799) the same system continued, but Napoleon ceased to protect Theophilanthropy. In 1801, though there seems to have been little discontent with the existing arrangement, Napoleon decided to upset it and bring the Pope upon the scene. The Catholic religion, as that of the majority, was again taken under the special protection of the State, the salaries of the clergy again paid by the nation, and the Papal authority over the Church again recognized within well-defined limits; while full toleration of other religions was maintained. This was the effect of the Concordat between the French Republic and the Pope. It is the judgment of a high authority that the nation, if it had been consulted, would have pronounced against the change. It may be doubted whether this is true. But Napoleon's policy seems to have been prompted by the calculation that, using the Pope as an instrument, he could control the consciences of men, and more easily carry out his plans of empire.

Apart from its ecclesiastical policies and its experiments in new creeds based on the principles of rationalistic thinkers, the French Revolution itself has an interest, in connexion with our subject, as an example of the coercion of reason by an intolerant faith.

The leaders believed that, by applying certain principles, they could regenerate France and show the world how the lasting happiness of mankind can be secured. They acted in the name of reason, but their principles were articles of faith, which were accepted just as blindly and irrationally as the dogmas of any supernatural creed. One of these dogmas was the false doctrine of Rousseau that man is a being who is naturally good and loves justice and order. Another was the illusion that all men are equal by nature. The puerile conviction prevailed that legislation could completely blot out the past and radically transform the character of a society. "Liberty, equality, and fraternity" was as much a creed as the Creed of the Apostles; it hypnotized men's minds like a revelation from on high; and reason had as little part in its propagation as in the spread of Christianity or of Protestantism. It meant anything but equality, fraternity, or liberty, especially liberty, when it was translated into action by the fanatical apostles of "Reason," who were blind to the facts of human nature and defied the facts of economics. Terror, the usual instrument in propagating religions, was never more mercilessly applied. Any one who questioned the doctrines was a heretic and deserved a heretic's fate. And, as in most religious movements, the milder and less unreasonable spirits succumbed to the fanatics. Never was the name of reason more grievously abused than by those who believed they were inaugurating her reign.

Religious liberty, however, among other good things, did emerge from the Revolution, at first in the form of Separation, and then under the Concordat. The Concordat lasted for more than a century, under monarchies and republics, till it was abolished in December, 1905, when the system of Separation was introduced again.

In the German States the history of religious liberty differs in many ways, but it resembles the development in France in so far as toleration in a limited form was at first brought about by war. The Thirty Years' War, which divided Germany in the first half of the seventeenth century, and in which, as in the English Civil War, religion and politics were mixed, was terminated by the Peace of Westphalia (1648). By this act, three religions, the Catholic, the Lutheran, and the Reformed [1] were legally recognized by the Holy Roman Empire, and placed on an equality; all other religions were excluded. But it was left to each of the German States, of which the Empire consisted, to tolerate or not any religion it pleased. That is, every prince could impose on his subjects whichever of the three religions he chose, and refuse to tolerate the others in his territory. But he might also admit one or both of the others, and he might allow the followers of other creeds to reside in his dominion, and practise their religion within the precincts of their own houses. Thus toleration varied, from State to State, according to the policy of each particular prince.

As elsewhere, so in Germany, considerations of political expediency promoted the growth of toleration, especially in Prussia; and as elsewhere, theoretical advocates exercised great influence on public opinion. But the case for toleration was based by its German defenders chiefly on legal, not, as in

[1] The Reformed Church consists of the followers of Calvin and Zwingli.

England and France, on moral and intellectual grounds. They regarded it as a question of law, and discussed it from the point of view of the legal relations between State and Church. It had been considered long ago from this standpoint by an original Italian thinker, Marsilius of Padua (thirteenth century), who had maintained that the Church had no power to employ physical coercion, and that if the lay authority punished heretics, the punishment was inflicted for the violation not of divine ordinances but of the law of the State, which excluded heretics from its territory.

Christian Thomasius may be taken as a leading exponent of the theory that religious liberty logically follows from a right conception of law. He laid down in a series of pamphlets (1693–1697) that the prince, who alone has the power of coercion, has no right to interfere in spiritual matters, while the clergy step beyond their province if they interfere in secular matters or defend their faith by any other means than teaching. But the secular power has no legal right to coerce heretics unless heresy is a crime. And heresy is not a crime, but an error; for it is not a matter of will. Thomasius, moreover, urges the view that the public welfare has nothing to gain from unity of faith, that it makes no

difference what faith a man professes so long as
he is loyal to the State. His toleration indeed
is not complete. He was much influenced by
the writings of his contemporary Locke, and
he excepts from the benefit of toleration the
same classes which Locke excepted.

Besides the influence of the jurists, we
may note that the Pietistic movement—a
reaction of religious enthusiasm against the
formal theology of the Lutheran divines—was
animated by a spirit favourable to toleration;
and that the cause was promoted by the
leading men of letters, especially by Lessing,
in the second half of the eighteenth century.

But perhaps the most important fact of
all in hastening the realization of religious
liberty in Germany was the accession of a
rationalist to the throne of Prussia, in the
person of Frederick the Great. A few months
after his accession (1740) he wrote in the
margin of a State paper, in which a question
of religious policy occurred, that every one
should be allowed to get to heaven in his own
way. His view that morality was independent of religion and therefore compatible
with all religions, and that thus a man could
be a good citizen—the only thing which the
State was entitled to demand—whatever
faith he might profess, led to the logical consequence of complete religious liberty. Cath-

olics were placed on an equality with Protestants, and the Treaty of Westphalia was violated by the extension of full toleration to all the forbidden sects. Frederick even conceived the idea of introducing Mohammedan settlers into some parts of his realm. Contrast England under George III, France under Louis XV, Italy under the shadow of the Popes. It is an important fact in history, which has hardly been duly emphasized, that full *religious* liberty was for the first time, in any country in modern Europe, realized under a free-thinking ruler, the friend of the great "blasphemer" Voltaire.

The policy and principles of Frederick were formulated in the Prussian Territorial Code of 1794, by which unrestricted liberty of conscience was guaranteed, and the three chief religions, the Lutheran, the Reformed, and the Catholic, were placed on the same footing and enjoyed the same privileges. The system is "jurisdictional"; only, three Churches here occupy the position which the Anglican Church alone occupies in England. The rest of Germany did not begin to move in the direction pointed out by Prussia until, by one of the last acts of the Holy Roman Empire (1803), the Westphalian settlement had been modified. Before the foundation of the new Empire (1870), freedom was established throughout Germany.

In Austria, the Emperor Joseph II issued an Edict of Toleration in 1781, which may be considered a broad measure for a Catholic State at that time. Joseph was a sincere Catholic, but he was not impervious to the enlightened ideas of his age; he was an admirer of Frederick, and his edict was prompted by a genuinely tolerant spirit, such as had not inspired the English Act of 1689. It extended only to the Lutheran and Reformed sects and the communities of the Greek Church which had entered into union with Rome, and it was of a limited kind. Religious liberty was not established till 1867.

The measure of Joseph applied to the Austrian States in Italy, and helped to prepare that country for the idea of religious freedom. It is notable that in Italy in the eighteenth century toleration found its advocate, not in a rationalist or a philosopher, but in a Catholic ecclesiastic, Tamburini, who (under the name of his friend Trautmansdorf) published a work *On Ecclesiastical and Civil Toleration* (1783). A sharp line is drawn between the provinces of the Church and the State, persecution and the Inquisition are condemned, coercion of conscience is declared inconsistent with the Christian spirit, and the principle is laid down that the sovran should only exercise coercion where

the interests of public safety are concerned.
Like Locke, the author thinks that atheism
is a legitimate case for such coercion.

The new States which Napoleon set up in
Italy exhibited toleration in various degrees,
but real liberty was first introduced in
Piedmont by Cavour (1848), a measure which
prepared the way for the full liberty which
was one of the first-fruits of the foundation
of the Italian kingdom in 1870.   The union of
Italy, with all that it meant, is the most
signal and dramatic act in the triumph of the
ideas of the modern State over the traditional
principles of the Christian Church.   Rome,
which preserved those principles most faithfully, has offered a steadfast, we may say a
heroic, resistance to the liberal ideas which
swept Europe in the nineteenth century.
The guides of her policy grasped thoroughly
the danger which liberal thought meant for
an institution which, founded in a remote
past, claimed to be unchangeable and never
out of date.   Gregory XVI issued a solemn
protest maintaining authority against freedom, the mediæval against the modern ideal,
in an Encyclical Letter (1832), which was
intended as a rebuke to some young French
Catholics (Lamennais and his friends) who
had conceived the promising idea of trans-
forming the Church by the Liberal spirit

of the day. The Pope denounces "the absurd and erroneous maxim, or rather insanity, that liberty of conscience should be procured and guaranteed to every one. The path to this pernicious error is prepared by that full and unlimited liberty of thought which is spread abroad to the misfortune of Church and State and which certain persons, with excessive impudence, venture to represent as an advantage for religion. Hence comes the corruption of youth, contempt for religion and for the most venerable laws, and a general mental change in the world—in short the most deadly scourge of society; since the experience of history has shown that the States which have shone by their wealth and power and glory have perished just by this evil—immoderate freedom of opinion, licence of conversation, and love of novelties. With this is connected the liberty of publishing any writing of any kind. This is a deadly and execrable liberty for which we cannot feel sufficient horror, though some men dare to acclaim it noisily and enthusiastically." A generation later Pius IX was to astonish the world by a similar manifesto—his Syllabus of Modern Errors (1864). Yet, notwithstanding the fundamental antagonism between the principles of the Church and the drift of modern civilization, the Papacy sur-

vives, powerful and respected, in a world
where the ideas which it condemned have
become the commonplace conditions of life.

The progress of Western nations from the
system of unity which prevailed in the fifteenth, to the system of liberty which was
the rule in the nineteenth century, was slow
and painful, illogical and wavering, generally
dictated by political necessities, seldom inspired by deliberate conviction. We have
seen how religious liberty has been realized,
so far as the law is concerned, under two
distinct systems, "Jurisdiction" and "Separation." But legal toleration may coexist
with much practical intolerance, and liberty
before the law is compatible with serious
disabilities of which the law cannot take
account. For instance, the expression of
unorthodox opinions may exclude a man from
obtaining a secular post or hinder his advancement. The question has been asked, which
of the two systems is more favourable to the
creation of a tolerant social atmosphere?
Ruffini (of whose excellent work on *Religious
Liberty* I have made much use in this chapter) decides in favour of Jurisdiction. He
points out that while Socinus, a true friend
of liberty of thought, contemplated this
system, the Anabaptists, whose spirit was
intolerant, sought Separation. More impor-

tant is the observation that in Germany, England, and Italy, where the most powerful Church or Churches are under the control of the State, there is more freedom, more tolerance of opinion, than in many of the American States where Separation prevails. A hundred years ago the Americans showed appalling ingratitude to Thomas Paine, who had done them eminent service in the War of Independence, simply because he published a very unorthodox book. It is notorious that free thought is still a serious hindrance and handicap to an American, even in most of the Universities. This proves that Separation is not an infallible receipt for producing tolerance. But I see no reason to suppose that public opinion in America would be different, if either the Federal Republic or the particular States had adopted Jurisdiction. Given legal liberty under either system, I should say that the tolerance of public opinion depends on social conditions and especially on the degree of culture among the educated classes.

From this sketch it will be seen that toleration was the outcome of new political circumstances and necessities, brought about by the disunion of the Church through the Reformation. But it meant that in those States which granted toleration the opinion of

a sufficiently influential group of the governing class was ripe for the change, and this
new mental attitude was in a great measure
due to the scepticism and rationalism which
were diffused by the Renaissance movement,
and which subtly and unconsciously had
affected the minds of many who were sincerely devoted to rigidly orthodox beliefs;
so effective is the force of suggestion.   In the
next two chapters the advance of reason at
the expense of faith will be traced through
the seventeenth, eighteenth, and nineteenth
centuries.

CHAPTER VI

THE GROWTH OF RATIONALISM

(SEVENTEENTH AND EIGHTEENTH CENTURIES)

DURING the last three hundred years reason
has been slowly but steadily destroying Christian mythology and exposing the pretensions
of supernatural revelation.   The progress of
rationalism falls naturally into two periods.
(1) In the seventeenth and eighteenth centuries those thinkers who rejected Christian
theology and the book on which it relies were
mainly influenced by the inconsistencies,
contradictions, and absurdities which they
discovered in the evidence, and by the moral

difficulties of the creed. Some scientific facts were known which seemed to reflect on the accuracy of Revelation, but arguments based on science were subsidiary. (2) In the nineteenth century the discoveries of science in many fields bore with full force upon fabrics which had been constructed in a naïve and ignorant age; and historical criticism undermined methodically the authority of the sacred documents which had hitherto been exposed chiefly to the acute but unmethodical criticisms of common sense.

A disinterested love of facts, without any regard to the bearing which those facts may have on one's hopes or fears or destiny, is a rare quality in all ages, and it had been very rare indeed since the ancient days of Greece and Rome. It means the scientific spirit. Now in the seventeenth century we may say (without disrespect to a few precursors) that the modern study of natural science began, and in the same period we have a series of famous thinkers who were guided by a disinterested love of truth. Of the most acute minds some reached the conclusion that the Christian scheme of the world is irrational, and according to their temperament some rejected it, whilst others, like the great Frenchman Pascal, fell back upon an unreasoning act of faith. Bacon, who professed orthodoxy, was perhaps at heart a deist, but in any case the whole spirit of his writings was to exclude authority from the domain of scientific investigation which he did so much to stimulate. Descartes, illustrious not only as the founder of modern metaphysics but also by his original contributions to science, might seek to conciliate the ecclesiastical authorities—his temper was timid— but his philosophical method was a powerful incentive to rationalistic thought. The general tendency of superior intellects was to exalt reason at the expense of authority; and in England this principle was established so firmly by Locke, that throughout the theological warfare of the eighteenth century both parties relied on reason, and no theologian of repute assumed faith to be a higher faculty.

A striking illustration of the gradual encroachments of reason is the change which was silently wrought in public opinion on the subject of witchcraft. The famous efforts of James I to carry out the Biblical command, "Thou shalt not suffer a witch to live," were outdone by the zeal of the Puritans under the Commonwealth to suppress the wicked old women who had commerce with Satan. After the Restoration, the belief in witchcraft declined among educated people—though

some able writers maintained it—and there
were few executions. The last trial of a
witch was in 1712, when some clergymen in
Hertfordshire prosecuted Jane Wenham.
The jury found her guilty, but the judge,
who had summed up in her favour, was able
to procure the remission of her sentence;
and the laws against witchcraft were repealed
in 1735. John Wesley said with perfect
truth that to disbelieve in witchcraft is to
disbelieve in the Bible. In France and in
Holland the decline of belief and interest in
this particular form of Satan's activity was
simultaneous. In Scotland, where theology
was very powerful, a woman was burnt in
1722. It can be no mere coincidence that
the general decline of this superstition belongs
to the age which saw the rise of modern science and modern philosophy.

Hobbes, who was perhaps the most brilliant
English thinker of the seventeenth century,
was a freethinker and materialist. He had
come under the influence of his friend the
French philosopher Gassendi, who had revived materialism in its Epicurean shape.
Yet he was a champion not of freedom of
conscience but of coercion in its most un-
compromising form. In the political theory
which he expounded in *Leviathan*, the sovran
has autocratic power in the domain of doc-

trine, as in everything else, and it is the duty of subjects to conform to the religion which the sovran imposes. Religious persecution is thus defended, but no independent power is left to the Church. But the principles on which Hobbes built up his theory were rationalistic. He separated morality from religion and identified "the true moral philosophy" with the "true doctrine of the laws of nature." What he really thought of religion could be inferred from his remark that the fanciful fear of things invisible (due to ignorance) is the natural seed of that feeling which, in himself, a man calls religion, but, in those who fear or worship the invisible power differently, superstition. In the reign of Charles II Hobbes was silenced and his books were burned.

Spinoza, the Jewish philosopher of Holland, owed a great deal to Descartes and (in political speculation) to Hobbes, but his philosophy meant a far wider and more open breach with orthodox opinion than either of his masters had ventured on. He conceived ultimate reality, which he called God, as an absolutely perfect, *impersonal* Being, a substance whose nature is constituted by two "attributes"— thought and spatial extension. When Spinoza speaks of love of God, in which he considered happiness to consist, he means knowledge and contemplation of the order of nature, including human nature, which is subject to fixed, invariable laws. He rejects free-will and the "superstition," as he calls it, of final causes in nature. If we want to label his philosophy, we may say that it is a form of pantheism. It has often been described as atheism. <u>If atheism means, as I suppose in ordinary use it is generally taken to mean, rejection of a personal God, Spinoza was an atheist</u>. It should be observed that in the seventeenth and eighteenth centuries atheist was used in the wildest way as a term of abuse for freethinkers, and when we read of atheists (except in careful writers) we may generally assume that the persons so stigmatized were really deists, that is, they believed in a personal God but not in Revelation.[1]

Spinoza's daring philosophy was not in harmony with the general trend of speculation at the time, and did not exert any profound influence on thought till a much later period. The thinker whose writings appealed most to the men of his age and were most opportune and effective was John Locke, who professed more or less orthodox Anglicanism. His great contribution to philosophy is equivalent to a very powerful defence

[1] For the sake of simplicity I use "deist" in this sense throughout, though "theist" is now the usual term.

of reason against the usurpations of authority. The object of his *Essay on the Human Understanding* (1690) is to show that all knowledge is derived from experience. He subordinated faith completely to reason. While he accepted the Christian revelation, he held that revelation if it contradicted the higher tribunal of reason must be rejected, and that revelation cannot give us knowledge as certain as the knowledge which reason gives. "He that takes away reason to make room for revelation puts out the light of both; and does much what the same as if he would persuade a man to put out his eyes, the better to receive the remote light of an invisible star by a telescope." He wrote a book to show that the Christian revelation is not contrary to reason, and its title, *The Reasonableness of Christianity*, sounds the note of all religious controversy in England during the next hundred years. Both the orthodox and their opponents warmly agreed that reasonableness was the only test of the claims of revealed religion. It was under the direct influence of Locke that Toland, an Irishman who had been converted from Roman Catholicism, composed a sensational book, *Christianity Not Mysterious* (1696). He assumes that Christianity is true and argues that there can be no mysteries in it, because mysteries, that

is, unintelligible dogmas, cannot be accepted
by reason. And if a reasonable Deity gave a
revelation, its purpose must be to enlighten,
not to puzzle. The assumption of the truth
of Christianity was a mere pretence, as an
intelligent reader could not fail to see. The
work was important because it drew the
logical inference from Locke's philosophy,
and it had a wide circulation. Lady Mary
Wortley Montagu met a Turkish Effendi at
Belgrade who asked her for news of Mr.
Toland.

It is characteristic of this stage of the
struggle between reason and authority that
(excepting the leading French thinkers in
the eighteenth century) the rationalists, who
attacked theology, generally feigned to acknowledge the truth of the ideas which they
were assailing. They pretended that their
speculations did not affect religion; they
could separate the domains of reason and
of faith; they could show that Revelation
was superfluous without questioning it; they
could do homage to orthodoxy and lay
down views with which orthodoxy was irre-
concilable. The errors which they exposed
in the sphere of reason were ironically allowed
to be truths in the sphere of theology. The
mediæval principle of double truth and other
shifts were resorted to, in self-protection

against the tyranny of orthodoxy—though they did not always avail; and in reading much of the rationalistic literature of this period we have to read between the lines. Bayle is an interesting instance.

If Locke's philosophy, by setting authority in its place and deriving all knowledge from experience, was a powerful aid to rationalism, his contemporary Bayle worked in the same direction by the investigation of history. Driven from France (see above, p. 107), he lived at Amsterdam, where he published his *Philosophical Dictionary*. He was really a freethinker, but he never dropped the disguise of orthodoxy, and this lends a particular piquancy to his work. He takes a delight in marshalling all the objections which heretics had made to essential Christian dogmas. He exposed without mercy the crimes and brutalities of David, and showed that this favourite of the Almighty was a person with whom one would refuse to shake hands. There was a great outcry at this unedifying candour. Bayle, in replying, adopted the attitude of Montaigne and Pascal, and opposed faith to reason.

The theological virtue of faith, he said, consists in believing revealed truths simply and solely on God's authority. If you believe in the immortality of the soul for

philosophical reasons, you are orthodox, but
you have no part in faith. The merit of
faith becomes greater, in proportion as the
revealed truth surpasses all the powers of
our mind; the more incomprehensible the
truth and the more repugnant to reason, the
greater is the sacrifice we make in accepting
it, the deeper our submission to God. Therefore a merciless inventory of the objections
which reason has to urge against fundamental
doctrines serves to exalt the merits of faith.

The *Dictionary* was also criticized for
the justice done to the moral excellencies of
persons who denied the existence of God.
Bayle replies that if he had been able to find
any atheistical thinkers who lived bad lives,
he would have been delighted to dwell on
their vices, but he knew of none such. As
for the criminals you meet in history, whose
abominable actions make you tremble, their
impieties and blasphemies prove they believed in a Divinity. This is a natural consequence of the theological doctrine that the
Devil, who is incapable of atheism, is the
instigator of all the sins of men. For man's
wickedness must clearly resemble that of the
Devil and must therefore be joined to a belief in God's existence, since the Devil is not
an atheist. And is it not a proof of the infinite wisdom of God that the worst criminals

are not atheists, and that most of the atheists whose names are recorded have been honest men? By this arrangement Providence sets bounds to the corruption of man; for if atheism and moral wickedness were united in the same persons, the societies of earth would be exposed to a fatal inundation of sin.

There was much more in the same vein; and the upshot was, under the thin veil of serving faith, to show that the Christian dogmas were essentially unreasonable.

Bayle's work, marked by scholarship and extraordinary learning, had a great influence in England as well as in France. It supplied weapons to assailants of Christianity in both countries. At first the assault was carried on with most vigour and ability by the English deists, who, though their writings are little read now, did memorable work by their polemic against the authority of revealed religion.

The controversy between the deists and their orthodox opponents turned on the question whether the Deity of natural religion—the God whose existence, as was thought, could be proved by reason—can be identified with the author of the Christian revelation. To the deists this seemed impossible. The nature of the alleged revelation seemed inconsistent with the character of the God to whom reason pointed. The defenders of revelation, at least all the most competent, agreed with the deists in making reason supreme, and through this reliance on reason some of them fell into heresies. Clarke, for instance, one of the ablest, was very unsound on the dogma of the Trinity. It is also to be noticed that with both sections the interest of morality was the principal motive. The orthodox held that the revealed doctrine of future rewards and punishments is necessary for morality; the deists, that morality depends on reason alone, and that revelation contains a great deal that is repugnant to moral ideals. Throughout the eighteenth century morality was the guiding consideration with Anglican Churchmen, and religious emotion, finding no satisfaction within the Church, was driven, as it were, outside, and sought an outlet in the Methodism of Wesley and Whitefield.

Spinoza had laid down the principle that Scripture must be interpreted like any other book (1670),[1] and with the deists this principle was fundamental. In order to avoid persecution they generally veiled their con-

---

[1] Spinoza's *Theological Political Treatise*, which deals with the interpretation of Scripture, was translated into English in 1689.

clusions under sufficiently thin disguises. Hitherto the Press Licensing Act (1662) had very effectually prevented the publication of heterodox works, and it is from orthodox works denouncing infidel opinions that we know how rationalism was spreading. But in 1695, the Press Law was allowed to drop, and immediately deistic literature began to appear. There was, however, the danger of prosecution under the Blasphemy laws. There were three legal weapons for coercing those who attacked Christianity: (1) The Ecclesiastical Courts had and have the power of imprisoning for a maximum term of six months, for atheism, blasphemy, heresy, and damnable opinions. (2) The common law as interpreted by Lord Chief Justice Hale in 1676, when a certain Taylor was charged with having said that religion was a cheat and blasphemed against Christ. The accused was condemned to a fine and the pillory by the Judge, who ruled that the Court of King's Bench has jurisdiction in such a case, inasmuch as blasphemous words of the kind are an offence against the laws and the State, and to speak against Christianity is to speak in subversion of the law, since Christianity is "parcel of the laws of England." (3) The statute of 1698 enacts that if any person educated in the Christian religion "shall by writing, printing, teaching, or advised speaking deny any one of the persons in the Holy Trinity to be God, or shall assert or maintain there are more gods than one, or shall deny the Christian religion to be true, or shall deny the Holy Scriptures of the Old and New Testament to be of divine authority," is convicted, he shall for the first offence be adjudged incapable to hold any public offices or employments, and on the second shall lose his civil rights and be imprisoned for three years. This Statute expressly states as its motive the fact that "many persons have of late years openly avowed and published many blasphemous and impious opinions contrary to the doctrine and principles of the Christian religion."

As a matter of fact, most trials for blasphemy during the past two hundred years fall under the second head. But the new Statute of 1698 was very intimidating, and we can easily understand how it drove heterodox writers to ambiguous disguises. One of these disguises was allegorical interpretation of Scripture. They showed that literal interpretation led to absurdities or to inconsistencies with the wisdom and justice of God, and pretended to infer that allegorical interpretation must be substituted. But they meant the reader to reject their pretended solution and draw a conclusion damaging to Revelation.

Among the arguments used in favour of the truth of Revelation the fulfilment of prophecies and the miracles of the New Testament were conspicuous. Anthony Collins, a country gentleman who was a disciple of Locke, published in 1733 his *Discourse on the Grounds and Reasons of the Christian Religion*, in which he drastically exposed the weakness of the evidence for fulfilment of prophecy, depending as it does on forced and unnatural figurative interpretations. Twenty years before he had written a *Discourse of Freethinking* (in which Bayle's influence is evident) pleading for free discussion and the reference of all religious questions to reason. He complained of the general intolerance which prevailed; but the same facts which testify to intolerance testify also to the spread of unbelief.

Collins escaped with comparative impunity, but Thomas Woolston, a Fellow of Sidney Sussex College, Cambridge, who wrote six aggressive *Discourses on the Miracles of our Saviour* (1727–1730) paid the penalty for his audacity. Deprived of his Fellowship, he was prosecuted for libel, and sentenced to a fine of £100 and a year's imprisonment. Unable to pay, he died in prison. He does

not adopt the line of arguing that miracles
are incredible or impossible. He examines
the chief miracles related in the Gospels,
and shows with great ability and shrewd
common sense that they are absurd or
unworthy of the performer. He pointed
out, as Huxley was to point out in a controversy with Gladstone, that the miraculous
driving of devils into a herd of swine was an
unwarrantable injury to somebody's property. On the story of the Divine blasting
of the fig tree, he remarks: "What if a yeo-
man of Kent should go to look for pippins in
his orchard at Easter (the supposed time that
Jesus sought for these figs) and because of a
disappointment cut down his trees? What
then would his neighbours make of him?
Nothing less than a laughing-stock; and if
the story got into our Publick News, he
would be the jest and ridicule of mankind."

Or take his comment on the miracle of the
Pool of Bethesda, where an angel used to
trouble the waters and the man who first
entered the pool was cured of his infirmity.
"An odd and a merry way of conferring a
Divine mercy. And one would think that
the angels of God did this for their own
diversion more than to do good to mankind.
Just as some throw a bone among a kennel
of hounds for the pleasure of seeing them

quarrel for it, or as others cast a piece of money among a company of boys for the sport of seeing them scramble for it, so was the pastime of the angels here." In dealing with the healing of the woman who suffered from a bloody flux, he asks: "What if we had been told of the Pope's curing an haemorrhage like this before us, what would Protestants have said to it? Why, 'that a foolish, credulous, and superstitious woman had fancied herself cured of some slight indisposition, and the crafty Pope and his adherents, aspiring after popular applause, magnified the presumed cure into a miracle.' The application of such a supposed story of a miracle wrought by the Pope is easy; and if Infidels, Jews, and Mahometans, who have no better opinion of Jesus than we have of the Pope, should make it, there's no help for it."

Woolston professed no doubts of the inspiration of Scripture. While he argued that it was out of the question to suppose the miracles literally true, he pretended to believe in the fantastic theory that they were intended allegorically as figures of Christ's mysterious operations in the soul of man. Origen, a not very orthodox Christian Father, had employed the allegorical method, and Woolston quotes him in his favour. His

vigorous criticisms vary in value, but many
of them hit the nail on the head, and the
fashion of some modern critics to pass over
Woolston's productions as unimportant because they are "ribald" or "coarse," is
perfectly unjust. The pamphlets had an
enormous sale, and Woolston's notoriety is
illustrated by the anecdote of the "jolly
young woman" who met him walking abroad
and accosted him with "You old rogue, are
you not hanged yet?" Mr. Woolston answered, "Good woman, I know you not;
pray what have I done to offend you?"
"You have writ against my Saviour," she
said; "what would become of my poor sinful
soul if it was not for my dear Saviour?"

About the same time, Matthew Tindal (a
Fellow of All Souls) attacked Revelation
from a more general point of view. In his
Christianity as old as the Creation (1730) he
undertook to show that the Bible as a revelation is superfluous, for it adds nothing to
natural religion, which God revealed to man
from the very first by the sole light of reason.
He argues that those who defend Revealed
religion by its agreement with Natural
religion, and thus set up a double government of reason and authority, fall between
the two. "It's an odd jumble," he observes,
"to prove the truth of a book by the truth

of the doctrines it contains, and at the same time conclude those doctrines to be true because contained in that book." He goes on to criticize the Bible in detail. In order to maintain its infallibility, without doing violence to reason, you have, when you find irrational statements, to torture them and depart from the literal sense. Would you think that a Mohammedan was governed by his Koran, who on all occasions departed from the literal sense? "Nay, would you not tell him that his inspired book fell infinitely short of Cicero's uninspired writings, where there is no such occasion to recede from the letter?"

As to chronological and physical errors, which seemed to endanger the infallibility of the Scriptures, a bishop had met the argument by saying, reasonably enough, that in the Bible God speaks according to the conceptions of those to whom he speaks, and that it is not the business of Revelation to rectify their opinions in such matters. Tindal made this rejoinder:—

"Is there no difference between God's not rectifying men's sentiments in those matters and using himself such sentiments as needs be rectified; or between God's not mending men's logic and rhetoric where 't is defective and using such himself; or between God's not contradicting vulgar notions and confirming them by speaking according to them? Can infinite wisdom despair of gaining or keeping people's affections without having recourse to such mean acts?"

He exposes with considerable effect the monstrosity of the doctrine of exclusive salvation. Must we not consider, he asks, whether one can be said to be sent as a Saviour of mankind, if he comes to shut Heaven's gate against those to whom, before he came, it was open provided they followed the dictates of their reason? He criticizes the inconsistency of the impartial and universal goodness of God, known to us by the light of nature, with acts committed by Jehovah or his prophets. Take the cases in which the order of nature is violated to punish men for crimes of which they were not guilty, such as Elijah's hindering rain from falling for three years and a half. If God could break in upon the ordinary rules of his providence to punish the innocent for the guilty, we have no guarantee that if he deals thus with us in this life, he will not act in the same way in the life to come, "since if the eternal rules of justice are once broken how can we imagine any stop?" But the ideals of holiness and justice in the Old Testament are strange indeed. The holier men are represented to be, the more cruel they seem and the more addicted to cursing. How surprising to find the holy prophet Elisha cursing in the name of the Lord little children for calling him Bald-pate! And, what is still more surprising, two she-bears immediately devoured forty-two little children.

I have remarked that theologians at this time generally took the line of basing Christianity on reason and not on faith. An interesting little book, *Christianity not founded on Argument*, couched in the form of a letter to a young gentleman at Oxford, by Henry Dodwell (Junior), appeared in 1741, and pointed out the dangers of such confidence in reason. It is an ironical development of the principle of Bayle, working out the thesis that Christianity is essentially unreasonable, and that if you want to believe, reasoning is fatal. The cultivation of faith and reasoning produce contrary effects; the philosopher is disqualified for Divine influences by his very progress in carnal wisdom; the Gospel must be received with all the obsequious submission of a babe who has no other disposition but to learn his lesson. Christ did not propose his doctrines to investigation; he did not lay the arguments for his mission before his disciples and give them time to consider

calmly of their force, and liberty to deter-
mine as their reason should direct them; the
apostles had no qualifications for the task,
being the most artless and illiterate persons
living.   Dodwell exposes the absurdity of the
Protestant position.   To give all men liberty
to judge for themselves and to expect at the
same time that they shall be of the Preacher's
mind is such a scheme for unanimity as one
would scarcely imagine any one could be weak
enough to devise in speculation and much
less that any could ever be found hardy
enough to avow and propose it to practice.
The men of Rome "shall rise up in the judgment (of all considering persons) against this
generation and shall condemn it; for they
invented but the one absurdity of infallibility, and behold a greater absurdity than
infallibility is here."

I have still to speak of the (Third) Earl of
Shaftesbury, whose style has rescued his
writings from entire neglect. His special
interest was ethics. While the valuable
work of most of the heterodox writers of this
period lay in their destructive criticism of
supernatural religion, they clung, as we have
seen, to what was called natural religion—
the belief in a kind and wise personal God,
who created the world, governs it by natural
laws, and desires our happiness.   The idea

was derived from ancient philosophers and had been revived by Lord Herbert of Cherbury in his Latin treatise *On Truth* (in the reign of James I). The deists contended that this was a sufficient basis for morality and that the Christian inducements to good behaviour were unnecessary Shaftesbury in his *Inquiry concerning Virtue* (1699) debated the question and argued that the scheme of heaven and hell, with the selfish hopes and fears which they inspire, corrupts morality and that the only worthy motive for conduct is the beauty of virtue in itself. He does not even consider deism a necessary assumption for a moral code; he admits that the opinion of atheists does not undermine ethics. But he thinks that the belief in a good governor of the universe is a powerful support to the practice of virtue. He is a thorough optimist, and is perfectly satisfied with the admirable adaptation of means to ends, whereby it is the function of one animal to be food for another. He makes no attempt to reconcile the red claws and teeth of nature with the beneficence of its powerful artist. "In the main all things are kindly and well disposed." The atheist might have said that he preferred to be at the mercy of blind chance than in the hands of an autocrat who, if he pleased Lord Shaftesbury's sense

of order, had created flies to be devoured
by spiders. But this was an aspect of the
universe which did not much trouble thinkers
in the eighteenth century. On the other
hand, the character of the God of the Old
Testament roused Shaftesbury's aversion.
He attacks Scripture not directly, but by
allusion or with irony. He hints that if
there is a God, he would be less displeased
with atheists than with those who accepted
him in the guise of Jehovah. As Plutarch
said, "I had rather men should say of me
that there neither is nor ever was such a one
as Plutarch, than they should say 'There was
a Plutarch, an unsteady, changeable, easily
provokable and revengeful man.'" Shaftesbury's significance is that he built up a positive theory of morals, and although it had
no philosophical depth, his influence on
French and German thinkers of the eighteenth century was immense.

In some ways perhaps the ablest of the
deists, and certainly the most scholarly, was
Rev. Conyers Middleton, who remained
within the Church. He supported Christianity on grounds of utility. Even if it is an
imposture, he said, it would be wrong to destroy it. For it is established by law and it
has a long tradition behind it. Some traditional religion is necessary and it would

be hopeless to supplant Christianity by reason. But his writings contain effective arguments which go to undermine Revelation. The most important was his *Free Inquiry* into Christian miracles (1748), which put in a new and dangerous light an old question: At what time did the Church cease to have the power of performing miracles? We shall see presently how Gibbon applied Middleton's method.

The leading adversaries of the deists appealed, like them, to reason, and, in appealing to reason, did much to undermine authority. The ablest defence of the faith, Bishop Butler's *Analogy* (1736), is suspected of having raised more doubts than it appeased. This was the experience of William Pitt the Younger, and the *Analogy* made James Mill (the utilitarian) an unbeliever. The deists argued that the unjust and cruel God of Revelation could not be the God of nature; Butler pointed to nature and said, There you behold cruelty and injustice. The argument was perfectly good against the optimism of Shaftesbury, but it plainly admitted of the conclusion—opposite to that which Butler wished to establish—that a just and beneficent God does not exist. Butler is driven to fall back on the sceptical argument that we are extremely ignorant; that all things

are possible, even eternal hell fire; and that
therefore the safe and prudent course is to
accept the Christian doctrine. It may be
remarked that this reasoning, with a few
modifications, could be used in favour of other
religions, at Mecca or at Timbuctoo. He has,
in effect, revived the argument used by Pascal that if there is one chance in any very
large number that Christianity is true, it is
a man's interest to be a Christian; for, if it
prove false, it will do him no harm to have
believed it; if it prove true, he will be infinitely the gainer. Butler seeks indeed to
show that the chances in favour amount to
a probability, but his argument is essentially
of the same intellectual and moral value as
Pascal's. It has been pointed out that it
leads by an easy logical step from the Anglican to the Roman Church. Catholics and
Protestants (as King Henry IV of France
argued) agree that a Catholic may be saved;
the Catholics assert that a Protestant will be
damned; therefore the safe course is to embrace Catholicism.[1]

I have dwelt at some length upon some
of the English deists, because, while they
occupy an important place in the history of

---

[1] See Benn, *Rationalism in the Nineteenth Century*, vol. i,
p. 138 *seq.*, for a good exposure of the fallacies and sophis-
tries of Butler.

rationalism in England, they also supplied, along with Bayle, a great deal of the thought which, manipulated by brilliant writers on the other side of the Channel, captured the educated classes in France. We are now in the age of Voltaire. He was a convinced deist. He considered that the nature of the universe proved that it was made by a conscious architect, he held that God was required in the interests of conduct, and he ardently combated atheism. His great achievements were his efficacious labour in the cause of toleration, and his systematic warfare against superstitions. He was profoundly influenced by English thinkers, especially Locke and Bolingbroke. This statesman had concealed his infidelity during his lifetime except from his intimates; he had lived long as an exile in France; and his rationalistic essays were published (1754) after his death. Voltaire, whose literary genius converted the work of the English thinkers into a world-force, did not begin his campaign against Christianity till after the middle of the century, when superstitious practices and religious persecutions were becoming a scandal in his country. He assailed the Catholic Church in every field with ridicule and satire. In a little work called *The Tomb of Fanaticism* (written 1736, published 1767), he begins by observing that a man who accepts his religion (as most people do) without examining it is like an ox which allows itself to be harnessed, and proceeds to review the difficulties in the Bible, the rise of Christianity, and the course of Church history; from which he concludes that every sensible man should hold the Christian sect in horror. "Men are blind to prefer an absurd and sanguinary creed, supported by executioners and surrounded by fiery faggots, a creed which can only be approved by those to whom it gives power and riches, a particular creed only accepted in a small part of the world—to a simple and universal religion." In the *Sermon of the Fifty* and the *Questions of Zapata* we can see what he owed to Bayle and English critics, but his touch is lighter and his irony more telling. His comment on geographical mistakes in the Old Testament is: "God was evidently not strong in geography." Having called attention to the "horrible crime" of Lot's wife in looking backward, and her conversion into a pillar of salt, he hopes that the stories of Scripture will make us better, if they do not make us more enlightened. One of his favourite methods is to approach Christian doctrines as a person who had just heard of the existence of Christians or Jews for the first time in his life.

His drama, *Saul* (1763), which the police tried to suppress, presents the career of David, the man after God's own heart, in all its naked horror. The scene in which Samuel reproves Saul for not having slain Agag will give an idea of the spirit of the piece.

SAMUEL: God commands me to tell you that he repents of having made you king.

SAUL: God repents! Only they who commit errors repent. His eternal wisdom cannot be unwise. God cannot commit errors.

SAMUEL: He can repent of having set on the throne those who do.

SAUL: Well, who does not? Tell me, what is my fault?

SAMUEL: You have pardoned a king.

AGAG: What! Is the fairest of virtues considered a crime in Judea?

SAMUEL (to Agag): Silence! do not blaspheme. (To Saul). Saul, formerly king of the Jews, did not God command you by my mouth to destroy all the Amalekites, without sparing women, or maidens, or children at the breast?

AGAG: Your god—gave such a command! You are mistaken, you meant to say, your devil.

SAMUEL: Saul, did you obey God?

SAUL: I did not suppose such a command

was positive. I thought that goodness was the first attribute of the Supreme Being, and that a compassionate heart could not displease him.

SAMUEL: You are mistaken, unbeliever. God reproves you, your sceptre will pass into other hands.

Perhaps no writer has ever roused more hatred in Christendom than Voltaire. He was looked on as a sort of anti-Christ. That was natural; his attacks were so tremendously effective at the time. But he has been sometimes decried on the ground that he only demolished and made no effort to build up where he had pulled down. This is a narrow complaint. It might be replied that when a sewer is spreading plague in a town, we cannot wait to remove it till we have a new system of drains, and it may fairly be said that religion as practised in contemporary France was a poisonous sewer. But the true answer is that knowledge, and therefore civilization, are advanced by criticism and negation, as well as by construction and positive discovery. When a man has the talent to attack with effect falsehood, prejudice, and imposture, it is his duty, if there are any social duties, to use it.

For constructive thinking we must go to the other great leader of French thought,

Rousseau, who contributed to the growth of freedom in a different way. He was a deist, but his deism, unlike that of Voltaire, was religious and emotional. He regarded Christianity with a sort of reverent scepticism. But his thought was revolutionary and repugnant to orthodoxy; it made against authority in every sphere; and it had an enormous influence. The clergy perhaps dreaded his theories more than the scoffs and negations of Voltaire. For some years he was a fugitive on the face of the earth. *Émile*, his brilliant contribution to the theory of education, appeared in 1762. It contains some remarkable pages on religion, "the profession of faith of a Savoyard vicar," in which the author's deistic faith is strongly affirmed and revelation and theology rejected. The book was publicly burned in Paris and an order issued for Rousseau's arrest. Forced by his friends to flee, he was debarred from returning to Geneva, for the government of that canton followed the example of Paris. He sought refuge in the canton of Bern and was ordered to quit. He then fled to the principality of Neufchâtel which belonged to Prussia. Frederick the Great, the one really tolerant ruler of the age, gave him protection, but he was persecuted and calumniated by the local clergy, who but for Frederick would

have expelled him, and he went to England
for a few months (1766), then returning to
France, where he was left unmolested till
his death. The religious views of Rousseau
are only a minor point in his heretical speculations. It was by his daring social and
political theories that he set the world on
fire. His *Social Contract* in which these
theories were set forth was burned at Geneva.
Though his principles will not stand criticism
for a moment, and though his doctrine worked
mischief by its extraordinary power of turning
men into fanatics, yet it contributed to progress, by helping to discredit privilege and to
establish the view that the object of a State
is to secure the wellbeing of *all* its members.

Deism—whether in the semi-Christian
form of Rousseau or the anti-Christian form
of Voltaire—was a house built on the sand,
and thinkers arose in France, England, and
Germany to shatter its foundations. In
France, it proved to be only a half-way inn
to atheism. In 1770, French readers were
startled by the appearance of Baron D'Holbach's *System of Nature*, in which God's existence and the immortality of the soul were
denied and the world declared to be matter
spontaneously moving.

Holbach was a friend of Diderot, who had
also come to reject deism. All the leading

ideas in the revolt against the Church had a place in Diderot's great work, the *Encyclopædia*, in which a number of leading thinkers collaborated with him. It was not merely a scientific book of reference. It was representative of the whole movement of the enemies of faith. It was intended to lead men from Christianity with its original sin to a new conception of the world as a place which can be made agreeable and in which the actual evils are due not to radical faults of human nature but to perverse institutions and perverse education. To divert interest from the dogmas of religion to the improvement of society, to persuade the world that man's felicity depends not on Revelation but on social transformation—this was what Diderot and Rousseau in their different ways did so much to effect. And their work influenced those who did not abandon orthodoxy; it affected the spirit of the Church itself. Contrast the Catholic Church in France in the eighteenth and in the nineteenth century. Without the work of Voltaire, Rousseau, Diderot, and their fellow-combatants, would it have been reformed? "The Christian Churches" (I quote Lord Morley) "are assimilating as rapidly as their formulæ will permit, the new light and the more generous moral ideas and the higher spirituality of teachers who have abandoned all churches and who are systematically denounced as enemies of the souls of men."

In England the prevalent deistic thought did not lead to the same intellectual consequences as in France; yet Hume, the greatest English philosopher of the century, showed that the arguments commonly adduced for a personal God were untenable. I may first speak of his discussion on miracles in his *Essay on Miracles* and in his philosophical *Inquiry concerning Human Understanding* (1748). Hitherto the credibility of miracles had not been submitted to a general examination independent of theological assumptions. Hume, pointing out that there must be a uniform experience against every miraculous event (otherwise it would not merit the name of miracle), and that it will require stronger testimony to establish a miracle than an event which is not contrary to experience, lays down the general maxim that "no testimony is sufficient to establish a miracle unless the testimony is of such a kind that its falsehood would be more miraculous than the fact which it endeavours to establish." But, as a matter of fact, no testimony exists of which the falsehood would be a prodigy. We cannot find in history any miracle attested by a sufficient number of men of such unquestionable good sense, education, and learning, as to secure us against all delusion in themselves; of such undoubted integrity as to place them beyond all suspicion of any design to deceive others; of such credit in the eyes of mankind as to have a great deal to lose in case of their being detected in any falsehood, and at the same time attesting facts performed in such a public manner as to render detection unavoidable —all which circumstances are requisite to give us a full assurance in the testimony of men.

In the *Dialogues on Natural Religion* which were not published till after his death (1776), Hume made an attack on the "argument from design," on which deists and Christians alike relied to prove the existence of a Deity. The argument is that the world presents clear marks of design, endless adaptation of means to ends, which can only be explained as due to the deliberate plan of a powerful intelligence. Hume disputes the inference on the ground that a mere intelligent being is not a sufficient cause to explain the effect. For the argument must be that the system of the material world demands as a cause a corresponding system of interconnected ideas; but such a mental system would demand an explanation of *its* existence just as much as the material world; and thus we find ourselves committed to an endless series of causes. But in any case, even if the argument held, it would prove only the existence of a Deity whose powers, though superior to man's, might be very limited and whose workmanship might be very imperfect. For this world may be very faulty, compared to a superior standard. It may be the first rude experiment "of some infant Deity who afterwards abandoned it, ashamed of his lame performance"; or the work of some inferior Deity at which his superior would scoff; or the production of some old superannuated Deity which since his death has pursued an adventurous career from the first impulse which he gave it. An argument which leaves such deities in the running is worse than useless for the purposes of Deism or of Christianity.

The sceptical philosophy of Hume had less influence on the general public than Gibbon's *Decline and Fall of the Roman Empire*. Of the numerous freethinking books that appeared in England in the eighteenth century, this is the only one which is still a widely read classic. In what a lady friend of Dr. Johnson called "the two offensive chapters" (XV and XVI) the causes of the rise and success of Christianity are for the first time critically investigated as a simple historical phenomenon. Like most freethinkers of the

time Gibbon thought it well to protect himself and his work against the possibility of
prosecution by paying ironical lip-homage
to the orthodox creed. But even if there had
been no such danger, he could not have chosen
a more incisive weapon for his merciless
criticism of orthodox opinion than the irony
which he wielded with superb ease. Having
pointed out that the victory of Christianity
is obviously and satisfactorily explained by
the convincing evidence of the doctrine and
by the ruling providence of its great Author,
he proceeds "with becoming submission" to
inquire into the secondary causes. He traces
the history of the faith up to the time of
Constantine in such a way as clearly to suggest that the hypothesis of divine interpo-
sition is superfluous and that we have to
do with a purely human development. He
marshals, with ironical protests, the obvious
objections to the alleged evidence for supernatural control. He does not himself criticize Moses and the prophets, but he repro-
duces the objections which were made against
their authority by "the vain science of the
gnostics." He notes that the doctrine of
immortality is omitted in the law of Moses,
but this doubtless was a mysterious dispensa-
tion of Providence. We cannot entirely remove "the imputation of ignorance and

obscurity which has been so arrogantly cast
on the first proselytes of Christianity," but
we must "convert the occasion of scandal into
a subject of edification" and remember that
"the lower we depress the temporal condition
of the first Christians, the more reason we
shall find to admire their merit and success."

Gibbon's treatment of miracles from the
purely historical point of view (he owed a
great deal to Middleton, see above, p. 150)
was particularly disconcerting. In the early
age of Christianity "the laws of nature were
frequently suspended for the benefit of the
Church. But the sages of Greece and Rome
turned aside from the awful spectacle, and,
pursuing the ordinary occupations of life and
study, appeared unconscious of any alterations in the moral or physical government of
the world. Under the reign of Tiberius the
whole earth, or at least a celebrated province
of the Roman Empire, was involved in a
praeternatural darkness of three hours.
Even this miraculous event, which ought to
have excited the wonder, the curiosity, and
the devotion of mankind, passed without
notice in an age of science and history. It
happened during the lifetime of Seneca and
the elder Pliny, who must have experienced
the immediate effects, or received the earliest
intelligence, of the prodigy. Each of these

philosophers in a laborious work has recorded all the great phenomena of nature, earthquakes, meteors, comets, and eclipses, which his indefatigable curiosity could collect. Both the one and the other have omitted to mention the greatest phenomenon to which the mortal eye has been witness since the creation of the globe." How "shall we excuse the supine inattention of the pagan and philosophic world to those evidences which were presented by the hand of Omnipotence, not to their reason, but to their senses?"

Again, if every believer is convinced of the reality of miracles, every reasonable man is convinced of their cessation. Yet every age bears testimony to miracles, and the testimony seems no less respectable than that of the preceding generation. When did they cease? How was it that the generation which saw the last genuine miracles performed could not distinguish them from the impostures which followed? Had men so soon forgotten "the style of the divine artist"? The inference is that genuine and spurious miracles are indistinguishable. But the credulity or "softness of temper" among early believers was beneficial to the cause of truth and religion. "In modern times, a latent and even involuntary scepticism adheres to the most pious dispositions. Their admission of supernatural truths is much less an active consent than a cold and passive acquiescence. Accustomed long since to observe and to respect the invariable order of nature, our reason, or at least our imagination, is not sufficiently prepared to sustain the visible action of the Deity."

Gibbon had not the advantage of the minute critical labours which in the following century were expended on his sources of information, but his masterly exposure of the conventional history of the early Church remains in many of its most important points perfectly valid to-day. I suspect that his artillery has produced more effect on intelligent minds in subsequent generations than the archery of Voltaire. For his book became indispensable as the great history of the Middle Ages; the most orthodox could not do without it; and the poison must have often worked.

We have seen how theological controversy in the first half of the eighteenth century had turned on the question whether the revealed religion was consistent and compatible with natural religion. The deistic attacks, on this line, were almost exhausted by the middle of the century, and the orthodox thought that they had been satisfactorily answered. But it was not enough to show that the revelation is reasonable; it was necessary to prove that it is real and rests on a solid historical basis. This was the question raised in an acute form by the criticisms of Hume and Middleton (1748) on miracles. The ablest answer was given by Paley in his *Evidences of Christianity* (1794), <u>the only one of the apologies of that age which is still read, though it has ceased to have any value</u>. Paley's theology illustrates how orthodox opinions are coloured, unconsciously, by the spirit of the time. He proved (in his *Natural Theology*) the existence of God by the argument from design —without taking any account of the criticisms of Hume on that argument. Just as a watchmaker is inferred from a watch, so a divine workman is inferred from contrivances in nature. Paley takes his instances of such contrivance largely from the organs and constitution of the human body. His idea of God is that of an ingenious contriver dealing with rather obstinate material. Paley's "God" (Mr. Leslie Stephen remarked) "has been civilized like man; he has become scientific and ingenious; he is superior to Watt or Priestley in devising mechanical and chemical contrivances, and is therefore made in the image of that generation of which Watt and Priestley were conspicuous lights." When a God of this kind

See per contra Oakum — Evolution in religion & education

is established there is no difficulty about
miracles, and it is on miracles that Paley
bases the case for Christianity—all other arguments are subsidiary. And his proof of
the New Testament miracles is that the apostles who were eye-witnesses believed in them,
for otherwise they would not have acted and
suffered in the cause of their new religion.
Paley's defence is the performance of an able
legal adviser to the Almighty.

The list of the English deistic writers of
the eighteenth century closes with one whose
name is more familiar than any of his predecessors, Thomas Paine. A Norfolk man,
he migrated to America and played a leading
part in the Revolution. Then he returned to
England and in 1791 published his *Rights
of Man* in two parts. I have been considering, almost exclusively, freedom of thought
in religion, because it may be taken as the
thermometer for freedom of thought in general. At this period it was as dangerous
to publish revolutionary opinions in politics
as in theology. Paine was an enthusiastic
admirer of the American Constitution and a
supporter of the French Revolution (in which
also he was to play a part). His *Rights of
Man* is an indictment of the monarchical
form of government, and a plea for representative democracy. It had an enormous

sale, a cheap edition was issued, and the
government, finding that it was accessible
to the poorer classes, decided to prosecute.
Paine escaped to France, and received a brilliant ovation at Calais, which returned him
as deputy to the National Convention. His
trial for high treason came on at the end of
1792. Among the passages in his book, on
which the charge was founded, were these:
"All hereditary government is in its nature
tyranny." "The time is not very distant
when England will laugh at itself for sending
to Holland, Hanover, Zell, or Brunswick
for men" [meaning King William III and
King George I] "at the expense of a million
a year who understood neither her laws, her
language, nor her interest, and whose capacities would scarcely have fitted them for the
office of a parish constable. If government
could be trusted to such hands, it must be
some easy and simple thing indeed, and
materials fit for all the purposes may be
found in every town and village in England."
Erskine was Paine's counsel, and he made a
fine oration in defence of freedom of speech.

"Constraint," he said, "is the natural
parent of resistance, and a pregnant proof
that reason is not on the side of those who
use it. You must all remember, gentlemen,
Lucian's pleasant story: Jupiter and a coun-

tryman were walking together, conversing with great freedom and familiarity upon the subject of heaven and earth. The countryman listened with attention and acquiescence while Jupiter strove only to convince him; but happening to hint a doubt, Jupiter turned hastily around and threatened him with his thunder. 'Ah, ha!' says the countryman, 'now, Jupiter, I know that you are wrong; you are always wrong when you appeal to your thunder.' This is the case with me. I can reason with the people of England, but I cannot fight against the thunder of authority."

Paine was found guilty and outlawed. He soon committed a new offence by the publication of an anti-Christian work, *The Age of Reason* (1794 and 1796), which he began to write in the Paris prison into which he had been thrown by Robespierre. This book is remarkable as the first important English publication in which the Christian scheme of salvation and the Bible are assailed in plain language without any disguise or reserve. In the second place it was written in such a way as to reach the masses. And, thirdly, while the criticisms on the Bible are in the same vein as those of the earlier deists, Paine is the first to present with force the incongruity of the Christian scheme with the conception of the universe attained by astronomical science.

"Though it is not a direct article of the Christian system that this world that we inhabit is the whole of the inhabitable globe, yet it is so worked up therewith—from what is called the Mosaic account of the creation, the story of Eve and the apple, and the counterpart of that story, the death of the Son of God—that to believe otherwise (that is, to believe that God created a plurality of worlds at least as numerous as what we call stars) renders the Christian system of faith at once little and ridiculous, and scatters it in the mind like feathers in the air. The two beliefs cannot be held together in the same mind; and he who thinks that he believes both has thought but little of either."

As an ardent deist, who regarded nature as God's revelation, Paine was able to press this argument with particular force. Referring to some of the tales in the Old Testament, he says: "When we contemplate the immensity of that Being who directs and governs the incomprehensible *Whole*, of which the utmost ken of human sight can discover but a part, we ought to feel shame at calling such paltry stories the Word of God."

The book drew a reply from Bishop Watson, one of those admirable eighteenth-century divines, who admitted the right of private judgment and thought that argument

should be met by argument and not by force.
His reply had the rather significant title,
An Apology for the Bible. George III remarked that he was not aware that any apology was needed for that book. It is a weak
defence, but is remarkable for the concessions
which it makes to several of Paine's criticisms of Scripture—admissions which were
calculated to damage the doctrine of the infallibility of the Bible.

It was doubtless in consequence of the
enormous circulation of the *Age of Reason*
that a Society for the Suppression of Vice
decided to prosecute the publisher. Unbelief was common among the ruling class,
but the view was firmly held that religion
was necessary for the populace and that any
attempt to disseminate unbelief among the
lower classes must be suppressed. Religion
was regarded as a valuable instrument to keep
the poor in order. It is notable that of the
earlier rationalists (apart from the case of
Woolston) the only one who was punished
was Peter Annet, a schoolmaster, who tried
to popularize freethought and was sentenced
for diffusing "diabolical" opinions to the
pillory and hard labour (1763). Paine held
that the people at large had the right of access
to all new ideas, and he wrote so as to reach
the people. Hence his book must be sup-

pressed. At the trial (1797) the judge placed every obstacle in the way of the defence. The publisher was sentenced to a year's imprisonment.

This was not the end of Paine prosecutions. In 1811 a Third Part of the *Age of Reason* appeared, and Eaton the publisher was condemned to eighteen months' imprisonment and to stand in the pillory once a month. The judge, Lord Ellenborough, said in his charge, that "to deny the truths of the book which is the foundation of our faith has never been permitted." The poet Shelley addressed to Lord Ellenborough a scathing letter. "Do you think to convert Mr. Eaton to your religion by embittering his existence? You might force him by torture to profess your tenets, but he could not believe them except you should make them credible, which perhaps exceeds your power. Do you think to please the God you worship by this exhibition of your zeal? If so, the demon to whom some nations offer human hecatombs is less barbarous than the deity of civilized society!" In 1819 Richard Carlisle was prosecuted for publishing the *Age of Reason* and sentenced to a large fine and three years' imprisonment. Unable to pay the fine he was kept in prison for three years. His wife and sister, who carried on the busi-

ness and continued to sell the book, were
fined and imprisoned soon afterwards and a
whole host of shop assistants.

If his publishers suffered in England, the
author himself suffered in America where
bigotry did all it could to make the last years
of his life bitter.

The age of enlightenment began in Germany in the middle of the eighteenth century.   In most of the German States, thought
was considerably less free than in England.
Under Frederick the Great's father, the phi-
lospher Wolff was banished from Prussia for
according to the moral teachings of the
Chinese sage Confucius a praise which, it was
thought, ought to be reserved for Christianity.   He returned after the accession of
Frederick, under whose tolerant rule Prussia
was an asylum for those writers who suffered
for their opinions in neighbouring States.
Frederick, indeed, held the view which was
held by so many English rationalists of the
time, and is still held widely enough, that
freethought is not desirable for the multi-
tude, because they are incapable of understanding philosophy.   Germany felt the
influence of the English Deists, of the French
freethinkers, and of Spinoza; but in the
German rationalistic propaganda of this
period there is nothing very original or in-

teresting. The names of Edelmann and
Bahrdt may be mentioned. The works of
Edelmann, who attacked the inspiration of
the Bible, were burned in various cities, and
he was forced to seek Frederick's protection
at Berlin. Bahrdt was more aggressive than
any other writer of the time. Originally
a preacher, it was by slow degrees that he
moved away from the orthodox faith. His
translation of the New Testament cut short
his ecclesiastical career. His last years were
spent as an inn-keeper. His writings, for
instance his popular *Letters on the Bible*, must
have had a considerable effect, if we may
judge by the hatred which he excited among
theologians.

It was not, however, in direct rationalistic
propaganda, but in literature and philosophy, that the German enlightenment of this
century expressed itself. The most illustrious men of letters, Goethe (who was profoundly influenced by Spinoza) and Schiller,
stood outside the Churches, and the effect
of their writings and of the whole literary
movement of the time made for the freest
treatment of human experience.

One German thinker shook the world—the
philosopher Kant. His *Critic of Pure Reason*
demonstrated that when we attempt to prove
by the light of the intellect the existence of

God and the immortality of the Soul, we fall
helplessly into contradictions. His destructive criticism of the argument from design
and all natural theology was more complete
than that of Hume; and his philosophy,
different though his system was, issued in the
same practical result as that of Locke, to
confine knowledge to experience. It is true
that afterwards, in the interest of ethics, he
tried to smuggle in by a back-door the Deity
whom he had turned out by the front gate,
but the attempt was not a success. His
philosophy—while it led to new speculative
systems in which the name of God was used
to mean something very different from the
Deistic conception—was a significant step
further in the deliverance of reason from the
yoke of authority.

CHAPTER VII

THE PROGRESS OF RATIONALISM

(NINETEENTH CENTURY)

MODERN science, heralded by the researches of Copernicus, was founded in the
seventeenth century, which saw the demon-
stration of the Copernican theory, the discovery of gravitation, the discovery of the
circulation of the blood, and the foundation

of modern chemistry and physics. The true nature of comets was ascertained, and they ceased to be regarded as signs of heavenly wrath. But several generations were to pass before science became, in Protestant countries, an involuntary arch-enemy of theology. Till the nineteenth century, it was only in minor points, such as the movement of the earth, that proved scientific facts seemed to conflict with Scripture, and it was easy enough to explain away these inconsistencies by a new interpretation of the sacred texts. Yet remarkable facts were accumulating which, though not explained by science, seemed to menace the credibility of Biblical history. If the story of Noah's Ark and the Flood is true, how was it that beasts unable to swim or fly inhabit America and the islands of the Ocean? And what about the new species which were constantly being found in the New World and did not exist in the Old? Where did the kangaroos of Australia drop from? The only explanation compatible with received theology seemed to be the hypothesis of innumerable new acts of creation, later than the Flood. It was in the field of natural history that scientific men of the eighteenth century suffered most from the coercion of authority. Linnæus felt it in Sweden, Buffon

in France. Buffon was compelled to retract
hypotheses which he put forward about the
formation of the earth in his *Natural History*
(1749), and to state that he believed implicitly
in the Bible account of Creation.

At the beginning of the nineteenth century
Laplace worked out the mechanics of the
universe, on the nebular hypothesis. His
results dispensed, as he said to Napoleon,
with the hypothesis of God, and were duly
denounced. His theory involved a long
physical process before the earth and solar
system came to be formed; but this was not
fatal, for a little ingenuity might preserve
the credit of the first chapter of *Genesis*.
Geology was to prove a more formidable
enemy to the Biblical story of the Creation
and the Deluge. The theory of a French
naturalist (Cuvier) that the earth had repeatedly experienced catastrophes, each of
which necessitated a new creative act, helped
for a time to save the belief in divine intervention, and Lyell, in his *Principles of
Geology* (1830), while he undermined the assumption of catastrophes, by showing that
the earth's history could be explained by the
ordinary processes which we still see in op-
eration, yet held fast to successive acts of
creation. It was not till 1863 that he presented fully, in his *Antiquity of Man*, the

evidence which showed that the human race
had inhabited the earth for a far longer period
than could be reconciled with the record of
Scripture. That record might be adapted
to the results of science in regard not only to
the earth itself but also to the plants and
lower animals, by explaining the word "day"
in the Jewish story of creation to signify
some long period of time. But this way out
was impossible in the case of the creation of
man, for the sacred chronology is quite
definite. An English divine of the seventeenth century ingeniously calculated that
man was created by the Trinity on October
23, B.C. 4004, at 9 o'clock in the morning, and
no reckoning of the Bible dates could put the
event much further back. Other evidence
reinforced the conclusions from geology, but
geology alone was sufficient to damage ir-
retrievably the historical truth of the Jewish
legend of Creation. The only means of res-
cuing it was to suppose that God had created
misleading evidence for the express purpose of
deceiving man.

Geology shook the infallibility of the Bible,
but left the creation of some prehistoric Adam
and Eve a still admissible hypothesis. Here
however zoology stepped in, and pronounced
upon the origin of man. It was an old conjecture that the higher forms of life, including

man, had developed out of lower forms, and
advanced thinkers had been reaching the
conclusion that the universe, as we find it,
is the result of a continuous process, unbroken by supernatural interference, and
explicable by uniform natural laws. But
while the reign of law in the world of non-
living matter seemed to be established, the
world of life could be considered a field in
which the theory of divine intervention is
perfectly valid, so long as science failed to
assign satisfactory causes for the origination
of the various kinds of animals and plants.
The publication of Darwin's *Origin of Species*
in 1859 is, therefore, a landmark not only in
science but in the war between science and
theology. When this book appeared, Bishop
Wilberforce truly said that "the principle
of natural selection is incompatible with the
word of God," and theologians in Germany
and France as well as in England cried aloud
against the threatened dethronement of the
Deity. The appearance of the *Descent of
Man* (1871), in which the evidence for the
pedigree of the human race from lower
animals was marshalled with masterly force,
renewed the outcry. The Bible said that
God created man in his own image, Darwin
said that man descended from an ape.
The feelings of the orthodox world may be

expressed in the words of Mr. Gladstone: "Upon the grounds of what is called evolution God is relieved of the labour of creation, and in the name of unchangeable laws is discharged from governing the world." It was a discharge which, as Spencer observed, had begun with Newton's discovery of gravitation. If Darwin did not, as is now recognized, supply a complete explanation of the origin of species, his researches shattered the supernatural theory and confirmed the view to which many able thinkers had been led that development is continuous in the living as in the non-living world. Another nail was driven into the coffin of Creation and the Fall of Adam, and the doctrine of redemption could only be rescued by making it independent of the Jewish fable on which it was founded.

Darwinism, as it is called, has had the larger effect of discrediting the theory of the adaptation of means to ends in nature by an external and infinitely powerful intelligence. The inadequacy of the argument from design, as a proof of God's existence, had been shown by the logic of Hume and Kant; but the observation of the life-processes of nature shows that the very analogy between nature and art, on which the argument depends, breaks down. The impropriety of the analogy has been pointed out, in a telling way, by a German writer (Lange). If a man wants to shoot a hare which is in a certain field, he does not procure thousands of guns, surround the field, and cause them all to be fired off; or if he wants a house to live in, he does not build a whole town and abandon to weather and decay all the houses but one. If he did either of these things we should say he was mad or amazingly unintelligent; his actions certainly would not be held to indicate a powerful mind, expert in adapting means to ends. But these are the sort of things that nature does. Her wastefulness in the propagation of life is reckless. For the production of one life she sacrifices innumerable germs. The "end" is achieved in one case out of thousands; the rule is destruction and failure. If intelligence had anything to do with this bungling process, it would be an intelligence infinitely low. And the finished product, if regarded as a work of design, points to incompetence in the designer. Take the human eye. An illustrious man of science (Helmholtz) said, "If an optician sent it to me as an instrument, I should send it back with reproaches for the carelessness of his work and demand the return of my money." Darwin showed how the phenomena might be explained as events not brought about

intentionally, but due to exceptional con-
currences of circumstances.

The phenomena of nature are a system of
things which co-exist and follow each other
according to invariable laws. This deadly
proposition was asserted early in the nineteenth century to be an axiom of science.
It was formulated by Mill (in his *System of
Logic*, 1843) as the foundation on which
scientific induction rests. It means that at
any moment the state of the whole universe
is the effect of its state at the preceding
moment; the casual sequence between two
successive states is not broken by any arbi-
trary interference suppressing or altering the
relation between cause and effect. Some ancient Greek philosophers were convinced
of this principle; the work done by modern
science in every field seems to be a verification
of it. But it need not be stated in such an
absolute form. Recently, scientific men have
been inclined to express the axiom with more
reserve and less dogmatically. They are
prepared to recognize that it is simply a pos-
tulate without which the scientific compre-
hension of the universe would be impossible,
and they are inclined to state it not as a
law of causation—for the idea of causation
leads into metaphysics—but rather as uniformity of experience. But they are not

readier to admit exceptions to this uniformity than their predecessors were to admit exceptions to the law of causation.

The idea of development has been applied not only to nature, but to the mind of man and to the history of civilization, including thought and religion. The first who attempted to apply this idea methodically to the whole universe was not a student of natural science, but a metaphysician, Hegel. His extremely difficult philosophy had such a wide influence on thought that a few words must be said about its tendency. He conceived the whole of existence as what he called the Absolute Idea, which is not in space or time and is compelled by the laws of its being to manifest itself in the process of the world, first externalizing itself in nature, and then becoming conscious of itself as spirit in individual minds. His system is hence called Absolute Idealism. The attraction which it exercised has probably been in great measure due to the fact that it was in harmony with nineteenth-century thought, in so far as it conceived the process of the world, both in nature and spirit, as a necessary development from lower to higher stages. In this respect indeed Hegel's vision was limited. He treats the process as if it were practically complete already, and does not take into account the probability of further development in the future, to which other thinkers of his own time were turning their attention. But what concerns us here is that, while Hegel's system is "idealistic," finding the explanation of the universe in thought and not in matter, it tended as powerfully as any materialistic system to subvert orthodox beliefs. It is true that some have claimed it as supporting Christianity. A certain colour is lent to this by Hegel's view that the Christian creed, as the highest religion, contains doctrines which express imperfectly some of the ideas of the highest philosophy—his own; along with the fact that he sometimes speaks of the Absolute Idea as if it were a person, though personality would be a limitation inconsistent with his conception of it. But it is sufficient to observe that, whatever value be assigned to Christianity, he regarded it from the *superior* standpoint of a purely intellectual philosophy, not as a special revelation of truth, but as a certain approximation to the truth which philosophy alone can reach; and it may be said with some confidence that any one who comes under Hegel's spell feels that he is in possession of a theory of the universe which relieves him from the need or desire of any revealed religion. His influence in Germany, Russia, and elsewhere has entirely made for highly unorthodox thought.

Hegel was not aggressive, he was superior. His French contemporary, Comte, who also thought out a comprehensive system, aggressively and explicitly rejected theology as an obsolete way of explaining the universe. He rejected metaphysics likewise, and all that Hegel stood for, as equally useless, on the ground that metaphysicians explain nothing, but merely describe phenomena in abstract terms, and that questions about the origin of the world and why it exists are quite beyond the reach of reason. Both theology and metaphysics are superseded by science—the investigation of causes and effects and co-existences; and the future progress of society will be guided by the scientific view of the world which confines itself to the positive data of experience. Comte was convinced that religion is a social necessity, and, to supply the place of the theological religions which he pronounced to be doomed, he invented a new religion—the religion of Humanity. It differs from the great religions of the world in having no supernatural or non-rational articles of belief, and on that account he had few adherents. But the "Positive Philosophy" of Comte has exercised great influence, not least in England, where its principles have been promulgated especially by Mr. Frederic Harrison, who in the latter half of the nineteenth century has been one of the most indefatigable workers in the cause of reason against authority.

Another comprehensive system was worked out by an Englishman, Herbert Spencer. Like Comte's, it was based on science, and attempts to show how, starting with a nebular universe, the whole knowable world, psychical and social as well as physical, can be deduced. His *Synthetic Philosophy* perhaps did more than anything else to make the idea of evolution familiar in England.

I must mention one other modern explanation of the world, that of Haeckel, the zoologist, professor at Jena, who may be called the prophet of evolution. His *Creation of Man* (1868) covered the same ground as Darwin's *Descent*, had an enormous circulation, and was translated, I believe, into fourteen languages. His *World-riddles* (1899) enjoys the same popularity. He has taught, like Spencer, that the principle of evolution applies not only to the history of nature, but also to human civilization and human thought. He differs from Spencer and Comte in not assuming any unknowable reality behind natural phenomena. His adversaries commonly stigmatize his theory as materialism, but this is a mistake. Like Spinoza he recognizes matter and mind, body and thought, as

two inseparable sides of ultimate reality,
which he calls God; in fact, he identifies his
philosophy with that of Spinoza. And he
logically proceeds to conceive material atoms
as thinking. His idea of the physical world
is based on the old mechanical conception
of matter, which in recent years has been
discredited. But Haeckel's *Monism*,[1] as he
called his doctrine, has lately been reshaped
and in its new form promises to exercise wide
influence on thoughtful people in Germany.
I will return later to this Monistic movement.

It had been a fundamental principle of
Comte that human actions and human history
are as strictly subject as nature is, to the law
of causation. Two psychological works appeared in England in 1855 (Bain's *Senses and
Intellect* and Spencer's *Principles of Psychology*), which taught that our volitions are
completely determined, being the inevitable
consequences of chains of causes and effects.
But a far deeper impression was produced
two years later by the first volume of Buckle's
History of Civilization in England (a work of
much less permanent value), which attempted
to apply this principle to history. Men act in
consequence of motives; their motives are
the results of preceding facts; so that "if we
were acquainted with the whole of the ante-

[1] From Greek *monos*, alone.

cedents and with all the laws of their movements, we could with unerring certainty
predict the whole of their immediate results."
Thus history is an unbroken chain of causes
and effects.   Chance is excluded; it is a mere
name for the defects of our knowledge.
Mysterious and providential interference is
excluded.   Buckle maintained God's existence, but eliminated him from history; and
his book dealt a resounding blow at the theory
that human actions are not submitted to the
law of universal causation.

The science of anthropology has in recent
years aroused wide interest.   Inquiries into
the condition of early man have shown
(independently of Darwinism) that there is
nothing to be said for the view that he fell
from a higher to a lower state; the evidence
points to a slow rise from mere animality.
The origin of religious beliefs has been investigated, with results disquieting for orthodoxy.
The researches of students of anthropology
and comparative religion—such as Tylor,
Robertson Smith, and Frazer—have gone
to show that mysterious ideas and dogma
and rites which were held to be peculiar to
the Christian revelation are derived from
the crude ideas of primitive religions.   That
the mystery of the Eucharist comes from the
common savage rite of eating a dead god,

that the death and resurrection of a god in human form, which form the central fact of Christianity, and the miraculous birth of a Saviour are features which it has in common with pagan religions—such conclusions are supremely unedifying. It may be said that in themselves they are not fatal to the claims of the current theology. It may be held, for instance, that, as part of Christian revelation, such ideas acquired a new significance and that God wisely availed himself of familiar beliefs—which, though false and leading to cruel practices, he himself had inspired and permitted—in order to construct a scheme of redemption which should appeal to the prejudices of man. Some minds may find satisfaction in this sort of explanation, but it may be suspected that most of the few who study modern researches into the origin of religious beliefs will feel the lines which were supposed to mark off the Christian from all other faiths dissolving before their eyes.

The general result of the advance of science, including anthropology, has been to create a coherent view of the world, in which the Christian scheme, based on the notions of an unscientific age and on the arrogant assumption that the universe was made for man, has no suitable or reasonable place. If Paine felt this a hundred years ago, it is far

more apparent now.   All minds however are
not equally impressed with this incongruity.
There are many who will admit the proofs
furnished by science that the Biblical record
as to the antiquity of man is false, but are
not affected by the incongruity between the
scientific and theological conceptions of the
world.

For such minds science has only succeeded
in carrying some entrenchments, which may
be abandoned without much harm.   It has
made the old orthodox view of the infallibility
of the Bible untenable, and upset the doctrine
of the Creation and Fall.   But it would still
be possible for Christianity to maintain the
supernatural claim, by modifying its theory
of the authority of the Bible and revising its
theory of redemption, if the evidence of
natural science were the only group of facts
with which it collided.   It might be argued
that the law of universal causation is a hypothesis inferred from experience, but that
experience includes the testimonies of history
and must therefore take account of the clear
evidence of miraculous occurrences in the
New Testament (evidence which is valid,
even if that book was not inspired).   Thus,
a stand could be taken against the generaliza-
tion of science on the firm ground of historical
fact.   That solid ground, however, has given

way, undermined by historical criticism, which has been more deadly than the common-sense criticism of the eighteenth century.

The methodical examination of the records contained in the Bible, dealing with them as if they were purely human documents, is the work of the nineteenth century. Something, indeed, had already been done. Spinoza, for instance (above, p. 138), and Simon, a Frenchman whose books were burnt, were pioneers; and the modern criticism of the Old Testament was begun by Astruc (professor of medicine at Paris), who discovered an important clue for distinguishing different documents used by the compiler of the Book of Genesis (1753). His German contemporary, Reimarus, a student of the New Testament, anticipated the modern conclusion that Jesus had no intention of founding a new religion, and saw that the Gospel of St. John presents a different figure from the Jesus of the other evangelists.

But in the nineteenth century the methods of criticism, applied by German scholars to Homer and to the records of early Roman history, were extended to the investigation of the Bible. The work has been done principally in Germany. The old tradition that the Pentateuch was written by Moses has been completely discredited. It is now

agreed unanimously by all who have studied
the facts that the Pentateuch was put together from a number of different documents
of different ages, the earliest dating from the
ninth, the last from the fifth, century B.C.;
and there are later minor additions. An
important, though undesigned, contribution
was made to this exposure by an Englishman, Colenso, Bishop of Natal. It had been
held that the oldest of the documents which
had been distinguished was a narrative which
begins in Genesis, Chapter I, but there was
the difficulty that this narrative seemed to
be closely associated with the legislation of
Leviticus which could be proved to belong to
the fifth century. In 1862 Colenso published
the first part of his *Pentateuch and the Book
of Joshua Critically Examined*. His doubts
of the truth of Old Testament history had
been awakened by a converted Zulu who
asked the intelligent question whether he
could really believe in the story of the Flood,
"that all the beasts and birds and creeping
things upon the earth, large and small, from
hot countries and cold, came thus by pairs
and entered into the ark with Noah? And
did Noah gather food for them *all*, for the
beasts and birds of prey as well as the rest?"
The Bishop then proceeded to test the accuracy of the inspired books by examining

the numerical statements which they contain. The results were fatal to them as historical records. Quite apart from miracles (the possibility of which he did not question), he showed that the whole story of the sojourn of the Israelites in Egypt and the wilderness was full of absurdities and impossibilities. Colenso's book raised a storm of indignation in England—he was known as "the wicked bishop"; but on the Continent its reception was very different. The portions of the Pentateuch and Joshua, which he proved to be unhistorical, belonged precisely to the narrative which had caused perplexity; and critics were led by his results to conclude that, like the Levitical laws with which it was connected, it was as late as the fifth century.

One of the most striking results of the researches on the Old Testament has been that the Jews themselves handled their traditions freely. Each of the successive documents, which were afterwards woven together, was written by men who adopted a perfectly free attitude towards the older traditions, and having no suspicion that they were of divine origin did not bow down before their authority. It was reserved for the Christians to invest with infallible authority the whole indiscriminate lump of these Jewish documents, inconsistent not only in their tendencies (since they reflect the spirit of different ages), but also in some respects in substance. The examination of most of the other Old Testament books has led to conclusions likewise adverse to the orthodox view of their origin and character. New knowledge on many points has been derived from the Babylonian literature which has been recovered during the last half century. One of the earliest (1872) and most sensational discoveries was that the Jews got their story of the Flood from Babylonian mythology.

Modern criticism of the New Testament began with the stimulating works of Baur and of Strauss, whose *Life of Jesus* (1835), in which the supernatural was entirely rejected, had an immense success and caused furious controversy. Both these rationalists were influenced by Hegel. At the same time a classical scholar, Lachmann, laid the foundations of the criticism of the Greek text of the New Testament, by issuing the first scientific edition. Since then seventy years of work have led to some certain results which are generally accepted.

In the first place, no intelligent person who has studied modern criticism holds the old view that each of the four biographies of Jesus is an independent work and an in-

dependent testimony to the facts which are
related. It is acknowledged that those portions which are common to more than one
and are written in identical language have the
same origin and represent only one testimony.
In the second place, it is allowed that the
first Gospel is not the oldest and that the
apostle Matthew was not its author. There
is also a pretty general agreement that Mark's
book is the oldest. The authorship of the
fourth Gospel, which like the first was supposed to have been written by an eye-witness,
is still contested, but even those who adhere
to the tradition admit that it represents a
theory about Jesus which is widely different
from the view of the three other biographers.

The result is that it can no longer be said
that for the life of Jesus there is the evidence
of eye-witnesses. The oldest account (Mark)
was composed at the earliest some thirty years
after the Crucifixion. If such evidence is
considered good enough to establish the
supernatural events described in that document, there are few alleged supernatural
occurrences which we shall not be equally
entitled to believe. As a matter of fact, an interval of thirty years makes little difference,
for we know that legends require little time
to grow. In the East, you will hear of
miracles which happened the day before

yesterday. The birth of religions is always enveloped in legend, and the miraculous thing would be, as M. Salomon Reinach has observed, if the story of the birth of Christianity were pure history.

Another disturbing result of unprejudiced examination of the first three Gospels is that, if you take the recorded words of Jesus to be genuine tradition, he had no idea of founding a new religion. And he was fully persuaded that the end of the world was at hand. At present, the chief problem of advanced criticism seems to be whether his entire teaching was not determined by this delusive conviction.

It may be said that the advance of knowledge has thrown no light on one of the most important beliefs that we are asked to accept on authority, the doctrine of immortality. Physiology and psychology have indeed emphasized the difficulties of conceiving a thinking mind without a nervous system. Some are sanguine enough to think that, by scientific examination of psychical phenomena, we may possibly come to know whether the "spirits" of dead people exist. If the existence of such a world of spirits were ever established, it would possibly be the greatest blow ever sustained by Christianity. For the great appeal of this and of some other re-

ligions lies in the promise of a future life of
which otherwise we should have no knowledge. If existence after death were proved
and became a scientific fact like the law of
gravitation, a revealed religion might lose
its power. For the whole point of a revealed religion is that it is not based on scientific facts. So far as I know, those who are
convinced, by spiritualistic experiments, that
they have actual converse with spirits of the
dead, and for whom this converse, however
delusive the evidence may be, is a fact proved
by experience, cease to feel any interest in
religion. They possess knowledge and can
dispense with faith.

The havoc which science and historical
criticism have wrought among orthodox
beliefs during the last hundred years was
not tamely submitted to, and controversy
was not the only weapon employed. Strauss
was deprived of his professorship at Tübingen,
and his career was ruined. Renan, whose
sensational *Life of Jesus* also rejected the
supernatural, lost his chair in the Collège de
France. Büchner was driven from Tübingen
(1855) for his book on *Force and Matter*,
which, appealing to the general public, set
forth the futility of supernatural explanations
of the universe. An attempt was made to
chase Haeckel from Jena. In recent years,

a French Catholic, the Abbé Loisy, has made notable contributions to the study of the New Testament and he was rewarded by major excommunication in 1907.

Loisy is the most prominent figure in a growing movement within the Catholic Church known as Modernism—a movement which some think is the gravest crisis in the history of the Church since the thirteenth century. The Modernists do not form an organized party; they have no programme. They are devoted to the Church, to its traditions and associations, but they look on Christianity as a religion which has developed, and whose vitality depends upon its continuing to develop. They are bent on reinterpreting the dogmas in the light of modern science and criticism. The idea of development had already been applied by Cardinal Newman to Catholic theology. He taught that it was a natural, and therefore legitimate, development of the primitive creed. But he did not draw the conclusion which the Modernists draw that if Catholicism is not to lose its power of growth and die, it must assimilate some of the results of modern thought. This is what they are attempting to do for it.

Pope Pius X has made every effort to suppress the Modernists. In 1907 (July) he

issued a decree denouncing various results of
modern Biblical criticism which are defended
in Loisy's works. The two fundamental
propositions that "the organic constitution
of the Church is not immutable, but that
Christian society is subject, like every human
society, to a perpetual evolution," and that
"the dogmas which the Church regards as
revealed are not fallen from heaven but are
an interpretation of religious facts at which
the human mind laboriously arrived"—both
of which might be deduced from Newman's
writings—are condemned. Three months
later the Pope issued a long Encyclical letter,
containing an elaborate study of Modernist
opinions, and ordaining various measures for
stamping out the evil. No Modernist would
admit that this document represents his
views fairly. Yet some of the remarks seem
very much to the point. Take one of their
books: "one page might be signed by a
Catholic; turn over and you think you are
reading the work of a rationalist. In writing
history, they make no mention of Christ's
divinity; in the pulpit, they proclaim it
loudly."

A plain man may be puzzled by these
attempts to retain the letter of old dogmas
emptied of their old meaning, and may think
it natural enough that the head of the Catho-

lic Church should take a clear and definite stand against the new learning which seems fatal to its fundamental doctrines. For many years past, liberal divines in the Protestant Churches have been doing what the Modernists are doing. The phrase "Divinity of Christ" is used, but is interpreted so as not to imply a miraculous birth. The Resurrection is preached, but is interpreted so as not to imply a miraculous bodily resurrection. The Bible is said to be an inspired book, but inspiration is used in a vague sense, much as when one says that Plato was inspired; and the vagueness of this new idea of inspiration is even put forward as a merit. Between the extreme views which discard the miraculous altogether, and the old orthodoxy, there are many gradations of belief. In the Church of England to-day it would be difficult to say what is the minimum belief required either from its members or from its clergy. Probably every leading ecclesiastic would give a different answer.

The rise of rationalism within the English Church is interesting and illustrates the relations between Church and State.

The pietistic movement known as Evangelicalism, which Wilberforce's *Practical View of Christianity* (1797) did much to make popular, introduced the spirit of Methodism within the Anglican Church, and soon put an end to the delightful type of eighteenth-century divine, who, as Gibbon says, "subscribed with a sigh or a smile" the articles of faith. The rigorous taboo of the Sabbath was revived, the theatre was denounced, the corruption of human nature became the dominant theme, and the Bible more a fetish than ever. The success of this religious "reaction," as it is called, was aided, though not caused, by the common belief that the French Revolution had been mainly due to infidelity; the Revolution was taken for an object lesson showing the value of religion for keeping the people in order. There was also a religious "reaction" in France itself. But in both cases this means not that free thought was less prevalent, but that the beliefs of the majority were more aggressive and had powerful spokesmen, while the eighteenth-century form of rationalism fell out of fashion. A new form of rationalism, which sought to interpret orthodoxy in such a liberal way as to reconcile it with philosophy, was represented by Coleridge, who was influenced by German philosophers. Coleridge was a supporter of the Church, and he contributed to the foundation of a school of liberal theology which was to make itself felt after the middle of the century.

Newman, the most eminent of the new High Church party, said that he indulged in a liberty of speculation which no Christian could tolerate. The High Church movement which marked the second quarter of the century was as hostile as Evangelicalism to the freedom of religious thought.

The change came after the middle of the century, when the effects of the philosophies of Hegel and Comte, and of foreign Biblical criticism, began to make themselves felt within the English Church. Two remarkable freethinking books appeared at this period which were widely read, F. W. Newman's *Phases of Faith* and W. R. Greg's *Creed of Christendom* (both in 1850). Newman (brother of Cardinal Newman) entirely broke with Christianity, and in his book he describes the mental process by which he came to abandon the beliefs he had once held. Perhaps the most interesting point he makes is the deficiency of the New Testament teaching as a system of morals. Greg was a Unitarian. He rejected dogma and inspiration, but he regarded himself as a Christian. Sir J. F. Stephen wittily described his position as that of a disciple "who had heard the Sermon on the Mount, whose attention had not been called to the Miracles, and who died before the Resurrection."

There were a few English clergymen (chiefly Oxford men) who were interested in German criticism and leaned to broad views, which to the Evangelicals and High Churchmen seemed indistinguishable from infidelity. We may call them the Broad Church—though the name did not come in till later. In 1855 Jowett (afterwards Master of Balliol) published an edition of some of St. Paul's Epistles, in which he showed the cloven hoof. It contained an annihilating criticism of the doctrine of the Atonement, an explicit rejection of original sin, and a rationalistic discussion of the question of God's existence. But this and some other unorthodox works of liberal theologians attracted little public attention, though their authors had to endure petty persecution. Five years later, Jowett and some other members of the small liberal group decided to defy the "abominable system of terrorism which prevents the statement of the plainest fact," and issued a volume of *Essays and Reviews* (1860) by seven writers of whom six were clergymen. The views advocated in these essays seem mild enough to-day, and many of them would be accepted by most well-educated clergymen, but at the time they produced a very painful impression. The authors were called the "Seven against Christ." It was

laid down that the Bible is to be interpreted
like any other book. "It is not a useful
lesson for the young student to apply to
Scripture principles which he would hesitate
to apply to other books; to make formal
reconcilements of discrepancies which he
would not think of reconciling in ordinary
history; to divide simple words into double
meanings; to adopt the fancies or conjectures
of Fathers and Commentators as real knowledge." It is suggested that the Hebrew
prophecies do not contain the element of
prediction. Contradictory accounts, or accounts which can only be reconciled by conjecture, cannot possibly have been dictated
by God. The discrepancies between the
genealogies of Jesus in Matthew and Luke,
or between the accounts of the Resurrection,
can be attributed "neither to any defect in
our capacities nor to any reasonable presumption of a hidden wise design, nor to any par-
tial spiritual endowments in the narrators."
The orthodox arguments which lay stress
on the assertion of witnesses as the supreme
evidence of fact, in support of miraculous
occurrences, are set aside on the ground that
testimony is a blind guide and can avail
nothing against reason and the strong grounds
we have for believing in permanent order.
It is argued that, under the Thirty-nine

Articles, it is permissible to accept as "parable or poetry or legend" such stories as that of an ass speaking with a man's voice, of waters standing in a solid heap, of witches and a variety of apparitions, and to judge for ourselves of such questions as the personality of Satan or the primeval institution of the Sabbath. The whole spirit of this volume is perhaps expressed in the observation that if any one perceives "to how great an extent the origin itself of Christianity rests upon *probable* evidence, his principle will relieve him from many difficulties which might otherwise be very disturbing. For relations which may repose on doubtful grounds as matters of history, and, as history, be incapable of being ascertained or verified, may yet be equally suggestive of true ideas with facts absolutely certain"—that is, they may have a spiritual significance although they are historically false.

The most daring Essay was the Rev. Baden Powell's *Study of the Evidences of Christianity*. He was a believer in evolution, who accepted Darwinism, and considered miracles impossible. The volume was denounced by the Bishops, and in 1862 two of the contributors, who were beneficed clergymen and thus open to a legal attack, were prosecuted and tried in the Ecclesiastical Court. Condemned on certain points, acquitted on others, they were sentenced to be suspended for a year, and they appealed to the Privy Council. Lord Westbury (Lord Chancellor) pronounced the judgment of the Judicial Committee of the Council, which reversed the decision of the Ecclesiastical Court. The Committee held, among other things, that it is not essential for a clergyman to believe in eternal punishment. This prompted the following epitaph on Lord Westbury: "Towards the close of his earthly career he dismissed Hell with costs and took away from Orthodox members of the Church of England their last hope of everlasting damnation."

This was a great triumph for the Broad Church party, and it is an interesting event in the history of the English State-Church. Laymen decided (overruling the opinion of the Archbishops of Canterbury and York) what theological doctrines are and are not binding on a clergyman, and granted within the Church a liberty of opinion which the majority of the Church's representatives regarded as pernicious. This liberty was formally established in 1865 by an Act of Parliament, which altered the form in which clergymen were required to subscribe the Thirty-nine Articles. The episode of *Essays and Reviews* is a landmark in the history of religious thought in England.

The liberal views of the Broad Churchmen and their attitude to the Bible gradually produced some effect upon those who differed most from them; and nowadays there is probably no one who would not admit, at least, that such a passage as Genesis, Chapter XIX, might have been composed without the direct inspiration of the Deity.

During the next few years orthodox public opinion was shocked or disturbed by the appearance of several remarkable books which criticized, ignored, or defied authority—Lyell's *Antiquity of Man*, Seeley's *Ecce Homo* (which the pious Lord Shaftesbury said was "vomited from the jaws of hell"), Lecky's *History of Rationalism*. And a new poet of liberty arose who did not fear to sound the loudest notes of defiance against all that authority held sacred. All the great poets of the nineteenth century were more or less unorthodox; Wordsworth in the years of his highest inspiration was a pantheist; and the greatest of all, Shelley, was a declared atheist. In fearless utterance, in unfaltering zeal against the tyranny of Gods and Governments, Swinburne was like Shelley. His drama *Atalanta in Calydon* (1865), even though a poet is strictly not answerable for what the persons in his drama say, yet with its denunciation of "the supreme evil, God," heralded the com-

ing of a new champion who would defy the
fortresses of authority. And in the following
year his *Poems and Ballads* expressed the
spirit of a pagan who flouted all the prejudices and sanctities of the Christian world.

But the most intense and exciting period
of literary warfare against orthodoxy in
England began about 1869, and lasted for
about a dozen years, during which enemies
of dogma, of all complexions, were less reticent
and more aggressive than at any other time
in the century. Lord Morley has observed
that "the force of speculative literature
always hangs on practical opportuneness,"
and this remark is illustrated by the rationalistic literature of the seventies. It was a
time of hope and fear, of progress and danger.
Secularists and rationalists were encouraged
by the Disestablishment of the Church in
Ireland (1869), by the Act which allowed
atheists to give evidence in a court of justice
(1869), by the abolition of religious tests at
all the universities (a measure frequently
attempted in vain) in 1871. On the other
hand, the Education Act of 1870, progressive
though it was, disappointed the advocates
of secular education, and was an unwelcome
sign of the strength of ecclesiastical influence.
Then there was the general alarm felt in
Europe by all outside the Roman Church,

and by some within it, at the decree of the
infallibility of the Pope (by the Vatican Council 1869–70), and an Englishman (Cardinal
Manning) was one of the most active spirits
in bringing about this decree. It would
perhaps have caused less alarm if the Pope's
denunciation of modern errors had not been
fresh in men's memories. At the end of 1864
he startled the world by issuing a Syllabus
"embracing the principal errors of our age."
Among these were the propositions, that every
man is free to adopt and profess the religion
he considers true, according to the light of
reason; that the Church has no right to
employ force; that metaphysics can and ought
to be pursued without reference to divine and
ecclesiastical authority; that Catholic states
are right to allow foreign immigrants to
exercise their own religion in public; that
the Pope ought to make terms with progress,
liberalism, and modern civilization. The
document was taken as a declaration of
war against enlightenment, and the Vatican
Council as the first strategic move of the hosts
of darkness. It seemed that the powers of
obscurantism were lifting up their heads with
a new menace, and there was an instinctive
feeling that all the forces of reason should be
brought into the field. The history of the
last forty years shows that the theory of

Infallibility, since it has become a dogma, is not more harmful than it was before. But the efforts of the Catholic Church in the years following the Council to overthrow the French Republic and to rupture the new German Empire were sufficiently disquieting. Against this was to be set the destruction of the temporal power of the Popes and the complete freedom of Italy. This event was the sunrise of Swinburne's *Songs before Sunrise* (which appeared in 1871), a seedplot of atheism and revolution, sown with implacable hatred of creeds and tyrants. The most wonderful poem in the volume, the *Hymn of Man*, was written while the Vatican Council was sitting. It is a song of triumph over the God of the priests, stricken by the doom of the Pope's temporal power. The concluding verses will show the spirit.

"By thy name that in hellfire was written, and burned at the point of thy sword,
Thou art smitten, thou God, thou art smitten; thy death is upon thee, O Lord.
And the lovesong of earth as thou diest resounds through the wind of her wings—
Glory to Man in the highest! for Man is the master of things."

The fact that such a volume could appear with impunity vividly illustrates the English policy of enforcing the laws for blasphemy only in the case of publications addressed to the masses.

Political circumstances thus invited and stimulated rationalists to come forward boldly, but we must not leave out of account the influence of the Broad Church movement and of Darwinism. The *Descent of Man* appeared precisely in 1871. A new, undogmatic Christianity was being preached in pulpits. Mr. Leslie Stephen remarked (1873) that "it may be said, with little exaggeration, that there is not only no article in the creeds which may not be contradicted with impunity, but that there is none which may not be contradicted in a sermon calculated to win the reputation of orthodoxy and be regarded as a judicious bid for a bishopric. The popular state of mind seems to be typified in the well-known anecdote of the cautious churchwarden, who, whilst commending the general tendency of his incumbent's sermon, felt bound to hazard a protest upon one point. 'You see, sir,' as he apologetically explained, 'I think there be a God.' He thought it an error of taste or perhaps of judgment, to hint a doubt as to the first article of the creed."

The influence exerted among the cultivated

classes by the æsthetic movement (Ruskin, Morris, the Pre-Raphaelite painters; then Pater's *Lectures on the Renaissance*, 1873) was also a sign of the times. For the attitude of these critics, artists, and poets was essentially pagan. The saving truths of theology were for them as if they did not exist. The ideal of happiness was found in a region in which heaven was ignored.

The time then seemed opportune for speaking out. Of the unorthodox books and essays,[1] which influenced the young and alarmed believers, in these exciting years, most were the works of men who may be most fairly described by the comprehensive term *agnostics*—a name which had been recently invented by Professor Huxley.

The agnostic holds that there are limits to human reason, and that theology lies outside those limits. Within those limits lies the world with which science (including psychology) deals. Science deals entirely with phenomena, and has nothing to say to the nature of the ultimate reality which may lie behind phenomena. There are four possible

[1] Besides the works referred to in the text, may be mentioned: Winwood Reade, *Martyrdom of Man*, 1871; Mill, *Three Essays on Religion;* W. R. Cassels, *Supernatural Religion;* Tyndall, *Address to British Association at Belfast;* Huxley, *Animal Automatism;* W. K. Clifford, *Body and Mind;* all in 1874.

attitudes to this ultimate reality. There is the attitude of the metaphysician and theologian, who are convinced not only that it exists but that it can be at least partly known. There is the attitude of the man who denies that it exists; but he must be also a metaphysician, for its existence can only be disproved by metaphysical arguments. Then there are those who assert that it exists but deny that we can know anything about it. And finally there are those who say that we cannot know whether it exists or not. These last are "agnostics" in the strict sense of the term, men who *profess not to know*. The third class go beyond phenomena in so far as they assert that there is an ultimate though unknowable reality beneath phenomena. But agnostic is commonly used in a wide sense so as to include the third as well as the fourth class—those who assume an unknowable, as well as those who do not know whether there is an unknowable or not. Comte and Spencer, for instance, who believed in an unknowable, are counted as agnostics. The difference between an agnostic and an atheist is that the atheist positively denies the existence of a personal God, the agnostic does not believe in it.

The writer of this period who held agnos-

ticism in its purest form, and who turned
the dry light of reason on to theological
opinions with the most merciless logic, was
Mr. Leslie Stephen. His best-known essay,
"An Agnostic's Apology" (*Fortnightly Review*, 1876), raises the question, have the
dogmas of orthodox theologians any meaning? Do they offer, for this is what we
want, an intelligible reconciliation of the
discords in the universe? It is shown in
detail that the various theological explanations of the dealings of God with man, when
logically pressed, issue in a confession of
ignorance. And what is this but agnosticism? You may call your doubt a mystery,
but mystery is only the theological phrase
for agnosticism. "Why, when no honest
man will deny in private that every ultimate problem is wrapped in the profoundest
mystery, do honest men proclaim in pulpits
that unhesitating certainty is the duty of
the most foolish and ignorant? We are
a company of ignorant beings, dimly dis-
cerning light enough for our daily needs,
but hopelessly differing whenever we attempt
to describe the ultimate origin or end of
our paths; and yet, when one of us ven-
tures to declare that we don't know the
map of the Universe as well as the map of
our infinitesimal parish, he is hooted, reviled,

and perhaps told that he will be damned to all eternity for his faithlessness." The characteristic of Leslie Stephen's essays is that they are less directed to showing that orthodox theology is untrue as that there is no reality about it, and that its solutions of difficulties are sham solutions. If it solved any part of the mystery, it would be welcome, but it does not, it only adds new difficulties. It is "a mere edifice of moonshine." The writer makes no attempt to prove by logic that ultimate reality lies outside the limits of human reason. He bases this conclusion on the fact that all philosophers hopelessly contradict one another; if the subject-matter of philosophy were, like physical science, within the reach of the intelligence, some agreement must have been reached.

The Broad Church movement, the attempts to liberalize Christianity, to pour its old wine into new bottles, to make it unsectarian and undogmatic, to find compromises between theology and science, found no favour in Leslie Stephen's eyes, and he criticized all this with a certain contempt. There was a controversy about the efficacy of prayer. Is it reasonable, for instance, to pray for rain? Here science and theology were at issue on a practical point which comes within the domain of science. Some theologians adopted the compromise that to pray against an eclipse would be foolish, but to pray for rain might be sensible. "One phenomenon," Stephen wrote, "is just as much the result of fixed causes as the other; but it is easier for the imagination to suppose the interference of a divine agent to be hidden away somewhere amidst the infinitely complex play of forces, which elude our calculations in meteorological phenomena, than to believe in it where the forces are simple enough to admit of prediction. The distinction is of course invalid in a scientific sense. Almighty power can interfere as easily with the events which are, as with those which are not, in the Nautical Almanac. One cannot suppose that God retreats as science advances, and that he spoke in thunder and lightning till Franklin unravelled the laws of their phenomena."

Again, when a controversy about hell engaged public attention, and some otherwise orthodox theologians bethought themselves that eternal punishment was a horrible doctrine and then found that the evidence for it was not quite conclusive and were bold enough to say so, Leslie Stephen stepped in to point out that, if so, historical

Christianity deserves all that its most viru-
lent enemies have said about it in this respect. When the Christian creed really
ruled men's consciences, nobody could utter
a word against the truth of the dogma of
hell. If that dogma had not an intimate
organic connection with the creed, if it had
been a mere unimportant accident, it could
not have been so vigorous and persistent
wherever Christianity was strongest. The
attempt to eliminate it or soften it down
is a sign of decline. "Now, at last, your
creed is decaying. People have discovered
that you know nothing about it; that
heaven and hell belong to dreamland; that
the impertinent young curate who tells me
that I shall be burnt everlastingly for not
sharing his superstition is just as ignorant
as I am myself, and that I know as much as
my dog. And then you calmly say again,
'It is all a mistake. Only believe in a something—and we will make it as easy for you
as possible. Hell shall have no more than
a fine equable temperature, really good for
the constitution; there shall be nobody in it
except Judas Iscariot and one or two others;
and even the poor Devil shall have a chance
if he will resolve to mend his ways.'"

Mr. Matthew Arnold may, I suppose, be
numbered among the agnostics, but he was

of a very different type. He introduced a
new kind of criticism of the Bible—literary
criticism. Deeply concerned for morality
and religion, a supporter of the Established
Church, he took the Bible under his special
protection, and in three works, *St. Paul and
Protestantism*, 1870, *Literature and Dogma*,
1873, and *God and the Bible*, 1875, he endeavoured to rescue that book from its orthodox
exponents, whom he regarded as the cor-
rupters of Christianity. It would be just,
he says, "but hardly perhaps Christian," to
fling back the word infidel at the orthodox
theologians for their bad literary and scientific criticisms of the Bible and to speak of
"the torrent of infidelity which pours every
Sunday from our pulpits!" The corruption
of Christianity has been due to theology
"with its insane licence of affirmation about
God, its insane licence of affirmation about
immortality"; to the hypothesis of "a magnified and non-natural man at the head of
mankind's and the world's affairs"; and the
fancy account of God "made up by putting
scattered expressions of the Bible together
and taking them literally." He chastises
with urbane persiflage the knowledge which
the orthodox think they possess about the
proceedings and plans of God. "To think
they know what passed in the Council of the

Trinity is not hard to them; they could easily think they even knew what were the hangings of the Trinity's council-chamber." Yet "the very expression, *the Trinity*, jars with the whole idea and character of Bible-religion; but, lest the Socinian should be unduly elated at hearing this, let us hasten to add that so too, and just as much, does the expression, a great Personal First Cause." He uses *God* as the least inadequate name for that universal order which the intellect feels after as a law, and the heart feels after as a benefit; and defines it as "the stream of tendency by which all things strive to fulfil the law of their being." He defined it further as a Power that makes for righteousness, and thus went considerably beyond the agnostic position. He was impatient of the minute criticism which analyzes the Biblical documents and discovers inconsistencies and absurdities, and he did not appreciate the importance of the comparative study of religions. But when we read of a dignitary in a recent Church congress laying down that the narratives in the books of Jonah and Daniel must be accepted because Jesus quoted them, we may wish that Arnold were here to reproach the orthodox for "want of intellectual seriousness."

These years also saw the appearance of

Mr. John Morley's sympathetic studies of the French freethinkers of the eighteenth century, *Voltaire* (1872), *Rousseau* (1873), and *Diderot* (1878). He edited the *Fortnightly Review*, and for some years this journal was distinguished by brilliant criticisms on the popular religion, contributed by able men writing from many points of view. A part of the book which he afterwards published under the title *Compromise* appeared in the *Fortnightly* in 1874. In *Compromise*, "the whole system of objective propositions which make up the popular belief of the day" is condemned as mischievous, and it is urged that those who disbelieve should speak out plainly. Speaking out is an intellectual duty. Englishmen have a strong sense of political responsibility, and a correspondingly weak sense of intellectual responsibility. Even minds that are not commonplace are affected for the worse by the political spirit which "is the great force in throwing love of truth and accurate reasoning into a secondary place." And the principles which have prevailed in politics have been adopted by theology for her own use. In the one case, convenience first, truth second; in the other, emotional comfort first, truth second. If the immorality is less gross in the case of religion, there is "the stain of intellectual improbity." And this is a crime against society, for "they who tamper with veracity from whatever motive are tampering with the vital force of human progress." The intellectual insincerity which is here blamed is just as prevalent to-day. The English have not changed their nature, the "political" spirit is still rampant, and we are ruled by the view that because compromise is necessary in politics it is also a good thing in the intellectual domain.

The *Fortnightly* under Mr. Morley's guidance was an effective organ of enlightenment. I have no space to touch on the works of other men of letters and of men of science in these combative years, but it is to be noted that, while denunciations of modern thought poured from the pulpits, a popular diffusion of freethought was carried on, especially by Mr. Bradlaugh in public lectures and in his paper, the *National Reformer*, not without collisions with the civil authorities.

If we take the cases in which the civil authorities in England have intervened to repress the publication of unorthodox opinions during the last two centuries, we find that the object has always been to prevent the spread of freethought among the masses.

The victims have been either poor, uneducated people, or men who propagated freethought in a popular form. I touched upon this before in speaking of Paine, and it is borne out by the prosecutions of the nineteenth and twentieth centuries. The unconfessed motive has been fear of the people. Theology has been regarded as a good instrument for keeping the poor in order, and unbelief as a cause or accompaniment of dangerous political opinions. The idea has not altogether disappeared that free thought is peculiarly indecent in the poor, that it is highly desirable to keep them superstitious in order to keep them contented, that they should be duly thankful for all the theological as well as social arrangements which have been made for them by their betters. I may quote from an essay of Mr. Frederic Harrison an anecdote which admirably expresses the becoming attitude of the poor towards ecclesiastical institutions. "The master of a workhouse in Essex was once called in to act as chaplain to a dying pauper. The poor soul faintly murmured some hopes of heaven. But this the master abruptly cut short and warned him to turn his last thoughts towards hell. 'And thankful you ought to be,' said he, 'that you have a hell to go to.'"

The most important English freethinkers who appealed to the masses were Holyoake,[1] the apostle of "secularism," and Bradlaugh. The great achievement for which Bradlaugh will be best remembered was the securing of the right of unbelievers to sit in Parliament without taking an oath (1888). The chief work to which Holyoake (who in his early years was imprisoned for blasphemy) contributed was the abolition of taxes on the Press, which seriously hampered the popular diffusion of knowledge.[2] In England, censorship of the Press had long ago disappeared (above, p. 139); in most other European countries it was abolished in the course of the nineteenth century.[3]

In the progressive countries of Europe there has been a marked growth of tolerance (I do not mean legal toleration, but the tol-

[1] It may be noted that Holyoake towards the end of his life helped to found the Rationalist Press Association, of which Mr. Edward Clodd has been for many years Chairman. This is the chief society in England for propagating rationalism, and its main object is to diffuse in a cheap form the works of freethinkers of mark (cp. Bibliography). I understand that more than two million copies of its cheap reprints have been sold.

[2] The advertisement tax was abolished in 1853, the stamp tax in 1855, the paper duty in 1861, and the optional duty in 1870.

[3] In Austria-Hungary the police have the power to suppress printed matter provisionally. In Russia the Press was declared free in 1905 by an Imperial decree, which, however, has become a dead letter. The newspapers are completely under the control of the police.

erance of public opinion) during the last
thirty years.   A generation ago Lord Morley
wrote: "The preliminary stage has scarcely
been reached—the stage in which public
opinion grants to every one the unrestricted
right of shaping his own beliefs, independently of those of the people who surround
him."   I think this preliminary stage has
now been passed.   Take England.   We are
now far from the days when Dr. Arnold
would have sent the elder Mill to Botany
Bay for irreligious opinions.   But we are
also far from the days when Darwin's *Descent*
created an uproar.   Darwin has been buried
in Westminster Abbey.   To-day books can
appear denying the historical existence of
Jesus without causing any commotion.   It
may be doubted whether what Lord Acton
wrote in 1877 would be true now: "There
are in our day many educated men who
think it right to persecute."   In 1895, Lecky
was a candidate for the representation of
Dublin University.   His rationalistic opinions were indeed brought up against him,
but he was successful, though the majority
of the constituents were orthodox.   In the
seventies his candidature would have been
hopeless.   The old commonplace that a
freethinker is sure to be immoral is no longer
heard.   We may say that we have now

reached a stage at which it is admitted by every one who counts (except at the Vatican), that there is nothing in earth or heaven which may not legitimately be treated without any of the assumptions which in old days authority used to impose.

In this brief review of the triumphs of reason in the nineteenth century, we have been considering the discoveries of science and criticism which made the old orthodoxy logically untenable. But the advance in freedom of thought, the marked difference in the general attitude of men in all lands towards theological authority to-day from the attitude of a hundred years ago, cannot altogether be explained by the power of logic. It is not so much criticism of old ideas as the appearance of new ideas and interests that changes the views of men at large. It is not logical demonstrations but new social conceptions that bring about a general transformation of attitude towards ultimate problems. Now the idea of the progress of the human race must, I think, be held largely answerable for this change of attitude. It must, I think, be held to have operated powerfully as a solvent of theological beliefs. I have spoken of the teaching of Diderot and his friends that man's energies should be devoted to making the earth pleasant. A

new ideal was substituted for the old ideal
based on theological propositions. It inspired the English Utilitarian philosophers
(Bentham, James Mill, J. S. Mill, Grote) who
preached the greatest happiness of the greatest number as the supreme object of action
and the basis of morality. This ideal was
powerfully reinforced by the doctrine of historical progress, which was started in France
(1750) by Turgot, who made progress the
organic principle of history. It was developed by Condorcet (1793), and put forward
by Priestley in England. The idea was
seized upon by the French socialistic philosophers, Saint-Simon and Fourier. The
optimism of Fourier went so far as to antici-
pate the time when the sea would be turned
by man's ingenuity into lemonade, when
there would be 37 million poets as great as
Homer, 37 million writers as great as Molière,
37 million men of science equal to Newton.
But it was Comte who gave the doctrine
weight and power. His social philosophy
and his religion of Humanity are based upon
it. The triumphs of science endorsed it; it
has been associated with, though it is not
necessarily implied in, the scientific theory
of evolution; and it is perhaps fair to say
that it has been the guiding spiritual force
of the nineteenth century. It has intro-

duced the new ethical principle of duty to
posterity. We shall hardly be far wrong if
we say that the new interest in the future
and the progress of the race has done a great
deal to undermine unconsciously the old
interest in a life beyond the grave; and it
has dissolved the blighting doctrine of the
radical corruption of man.

Nowhere has the theory of progress been
more emphatically recognized than in the
Monistic movement which has been exciting
great interest in Germany (1910–12). This
movement is based on the ideas of Haeckel,
who is looked up to as the master; but those
ideas have been considerably changed under
the influence of Ostwald, the new leader.
While Haeckel is a biologist, Ostwald's
brilliant work was done in chemistry and
physics. The new Monism differs from the
old, in the first place, in being much less
dogmatic. It declares that all that is in our
experience can be the object of a corresponding science. It is much more a method than
a system, for its sole ultimate object is to
comprehend all human experience in unified
knowledge. Secondly, while it maintains,
with Haeckel, evolution as the guiding principle in the history of living things, it rejects
his pantheism and his theory of thinking
atoms. The old mechanical theory of the

physical world has been gradually supplanted
by the theory of energy, and Ostwald, who
was one of the foremost exponents of energy,
has made it a leading idea of Monism.   What
has been called matter is, so far as we know
now, simply a complex of energies, and he
has sought to extend the "energetic" principle from physical or chemical to biological,
psychical, and social phenomena.   But it is
to be observed that no finality is claimed for
the conception of energy; it is simply an
hypothesis which corresponds to our present
stage of knowledge, and may, as knowledge
advances, be superseded.

Monism resembles the positive philosophy
and religion of Comte in so far as it means an
outlook on life based entirely on science and
excluding theology, mysticism, and metaphysics.   It may be called a religion, if we
adopt Mr. MacTaggart's definition of religion
as "an emotion resting on a conviction of
the harmony between ourselves and the
universe at large."   But it is much better not
to use the word religion in connexion with it,
and the Monists have no thought of finding
a Monistic, as Comte founded a Positivist,
church.   They insist upon the sharp opposition between the outlook of science and the
outlook of religion, and find the mark of
spiritual progress in the fact that religion is

gradually becoming less indispensable. The
further we go back in the past, the more
valuable is religion as an element in civilization; as we advance, it retreats more and
more into the background, to be replaced by
science. Religions have been, in principle,
pessimistic, so far as the present world is
concerned; Monism is, in principle, opti-
mistic, for it recognizes that the process of
his evolution has overcome, in increasing
measure, the bad element in man, and will go
on overcoming it still more. Monism pro-
claims that development and progress are
the practical principles of human conduct,
while the Churches, especially the Catholic
Church, have been steadily conservative,
and though they have been unable to put a
stop to progress have endeavoured to suppress its symptoms—to bottle up the steam.[1]
The Monistic congress at Hamburg in 1911
had a success which surprised its promoters.
The movement bids fair to be a powerful
influence in diffusing rationalistic thought.[2]

If we take the three large States of

[1] I have taken these points, illustrating the Monistic
attitude to the Churches, from Ostwald's *Monistic Sunday
Sermons* (German), 1911, 1912.

[2] I may note here that, as this is not a history of thought,
I make no reference to recent philosophical speculations
(in America, England, and France) which are sometimes
claimed as tending to bolster up theology. But they are
all profoundly unorthodox.

Western Europe, in which the majority of
Christians are Catholics, we see how the ideal
of progress, freedom of thought, and the
decline of ecclesiastical power go together.
In Spain, where the Church has enormous
power and wealth and can still dictate to the
Court and the politicians, the idea of progress, which is vital in France and Italy, has
not yet made its influence seriously felt.
Liberal thought indeed is widely spread in
the small educated class, but the great majority of the whole population are illiterate,
and it is the interest of the Church to keep
them so. The education of the people, as all
enlightened Spaniards confess, is the pressing need of the country. How formidable
are the obstacles which will have to be overcome before modern education is allowed to
spread was shown four years ago by the
tragedy of Francisco Ferrer, which reminded
everybody that in one corner of Western
Europe the mediæval spirit is still vigorous.
Ferrer had devoted himself to the founding
of modern schools in the province of Cata-
lonia (since 1901). He was a rationalist,
and his schools, which had a marked success,
were entirely secular. The ecclesiastical authorities execrated him, and in the summer
of 1909 chance gave them the means of
destroying him. A strike of workmen at

Barcelona developed into a violent revolution, Ferrer happened to be in Barcelona for some days at the beginning of the movement, with which he had no connection whatever, and his enemies seized the opportunity to make him responsible for it. False evidence (including forged documents) was manufactured. Evidence which would have helped his case was suppressed. The Catholic papers agitated against him, and the leading ecclesiastics of Barcelona urged the Government not to spare the man who founded the modern schools, the root of all the trouble. Ferrer was condemned by a military tribunal and shot (Oct. 13). He suffered in the cause of reason and freedom of thought, though, as there is no longer an Inquisition, his enemies had to kill him under the false charge of anarchy and treason. It is possible that the indignation which was felt in Europe and was most loudly expressed in France may prevent the repetition of such extreme measures, but almost anything may happen in a country where the Church is so powerful and so bigoted, and the politicians so corrupt.

CHAPTER VIII

THE JUSTIFICATION OF LIBERTY OF THOUGHT

Most men who have been brought up in the free atmosphere of a modern State sympathize with liberty in its long struggle with authority and may find it difficult to see that anything can be said for the tyrannical, and as they think extraordinarily perverse, policy by which communities and governments persistently sought to stifle new ideas and suppress free speculation. The conflict sketched in these pages appears as a war between light and darkness. We exclaim that altar and throne formed a sinister conspiracy against the progress of humanity. We look back with horror at the things which so many champions of reason endured at the hands of blind, if not malignant, bearers of authority.

But a more or less plausible case can be made out for coercion. Let us take the most limited view of the lawful powers of society over its individual members. Let us lay down, with Mill, that "the sole end for which mankind are warranted, individually and collectively, in interfering with the liberty of action of any of their members is self-protection," and that coercion is only justified for the prevention of harm to others. This is the minimum claim the State can make, and it will be admitted that it is not only the right but the duty of the State to prevent harm to its members. That is what it is for. Now no abstract or independent principle is discoverable, why liberty of speech should be a privileged form of liberty of action, or why society should lay down its arms of defence and fold its hands, when it is persuaded that harm is threatened to it through the speech of any of its members. The Government has to judge of the danger, and its judgment may be wrong; but if it is convinced that harm is being done, is it not its plain duty to interfere?

This argument supplies an apology for the suppression of free opinion by Governments in ancient and modern times. It can be urged for the Inquisition, for Censorship of the Press, for Blasphemy laws, for all coercive measures of the kind, that, if excessive or ill-judged, they were intended to protect society against what their authors sincerely believed to be grave injury, and were simple acts of duty. (This apology, of course, does not extend to acts done for the sake of the alleged good of the victims themselves, namely, to secure their future salvation.)

Nowadays we condemn all such measures

and disallow the right of the State to interfere with the free expression of opinion. So deeply is the doctrine of liberty seated in our minds that we find it difficult to make allowances for the coercive practices of our misguided ancestors. How is this doctrine justified? It rests on no abstract basis, on no principle independent of society itself, but entirely on considerations of utility.

We saw how Socrates indicated the social value of freedom of discussion. We saw how Milton observed that such freedom was necessary for the advance of knowledge. But in the period during which the cause of toleration was fought for and practically won, the argument more generally used was the injustice of punishing a man for opinions which he honestly held and could not help holding, since conviction is not a matter of will; in other words, the argument that error is not a crime and that it is therefore unjust to punish it. This argument, however, does not prove the case for freedom of discussion. The advocate of coercion may reply: We admit that it is unjust to punish a man for private erroneous beliefs; but it is not unjust to forbid the propagation of such beliefs if we are convinced that they are harmful; it is not unjust to punish him, not for holding them, but for publishing them. The truth is that, in examining principles, the word *just* is misleading. All the virtues are based on experience, physiological or social, and justice is no exception. *Just* designates a class of rules or principles of which the social utility has been found by experience to be paramount and which are recognized to be so important as to override all considerations of immediate expediency. And social utility is the only test. It is futile, therefore, to say to a Government that it acts unjustly in coercing opinion, unless it is shown that freedom of opinion is a principle of such overmastering social utility as to render other considerations negligible. Socrates had a true instinct in taking the line that freedom is valuable to society.

The reasoned justification of liberty of thought is due to J. S. Mill, who set it forth in his work *On Liberty*, published in 1859. This book treats of liberty in general, and attempts to fix the frontier of the region in which individual freedom should be considered absolute and unassailable. The second chapter considers liberty of thought and discussion, and if many may think that Mill unduly minimized the functions of society, underrating its claims as against the individual, few will deny the justice of the chief arguments or question the general soundness of his conclusions.

Pointing out that no fixed standard was recognized for testing the propriety of the interference on the part of the community with its individual members, he finds the test in self-protection, that is, the prevention of harm to others. He bases the proposition not on abstract rights, but on "utility, in the largest sense, grounded on the permanent interests of man as a progressive being." He then uses the following argument to show that to silence opinion and discussion is always contrary to those permanent interests. Those who would suppress an opinion (it is assumed that they are honest) deny its truth, but they are not infallible. They may be wrong, or right, or partly wrong and partly right. (1) If they are wrong and the opinion they would crush is true, they have robbed, or done their utmost to rob, mankind of a truth. They will say: But we were justified, for we exercised our judgment to the best of our ability, and are we to be told that because our judgment is fallible we are not to use it? We forbade the propagation of an opinion which we were sure was false and pernicious; this implies no greater claim to infallibility than any act done by public authority. If we are to act at all, we must assume our own opinion to be true. To this Mill acutely replies: "There is the greatest differ-

ence between assuming an opinion to be true,
because with every opportunity for contesting
it it has not been refuted, and assuming its
truth for the purpose of not permitting its
refutation.   Complete liberty of contradicting and disproving our opinion is the very
condition which justifies us in assuming its
truth for purposes of action, and on no other
terms can a being with human faculties have
any rational assurance of being right."

(2) If the received opinion which it is
sought to protect against the intrusion of
error is true, the suppression of discussion is
still contrary to general utility.   A received
opinion may happen to be true (it is very
seldom entirely true); but a rational certainty
that it is so can only be secured by the fact
that it has been fully canvassed but has not
been shaken.

Commoner and more important is (3) the
case where the conflicting doctrines share the
truth between them.   Here Mill has little
difficulty in proving the utility of supple-
menting one-sided popular truths by other
truths which popular opinion omits to consider.   And he observes that if either of the
opinions which share the truth has a claim
not merely to be tolerated but to be encouraged, it is the one which happens to be held
by the minority, since this is the one "which

for the time being represents the neglected interests." He takes the doctrines of Rousseau, which might conceivably have been suppressed as pernicious. To the self-complacent eighteenth century those doctrines came as "a salutary shock, dislocating the compact mass of one-sided opinion." The current opinions were indeed nearer to the truth than Rousseau's, they contained much less of error; "nevertheless there lay in Rousseau's doctrine, and has floated down the stream of opinion along with it, a considerable amount of exactly those truths which the popular opinion wanted; and these are the deposit which we left behind when the flood subsided."

Such is the drift of Mill's main argument. The present writer would prefer to state the justification of freedom of opinion in a somewhat different form, though in accordance with Mill's reasoning. The progress of civilization, if it is partly conditioned by circumstances beyond man's control, depends more, and in an increasing measure, on things which are within his own power. Prominent among these are the advancement of knowledge and the deliberate adaptation of his habits and institutions to new conditions. To advance knowledge and to correct errors, unrestricted freedom of discussion is required.

History shows that knowledge grew when speculation was perfectly free in Greece, and that in modern times, since restrictions on inquiry have been entirely removed, it has advanced with a velocity which would seem diabolical to the slaves of the mediæval Church. Then, it is obvious that in order to readjust social customs, institutions, and methods to new needs and circumstances, there must be unlimited freedom of canvassing and criticizing them, of expressing the most unpopular opinions, no matter how offensive to prevailing sentiment they may be. If the history of civilization has any lesson to teach it is this: there is one supreme condition of mental and moral progress which it is completely within the power of man himself to secure, and that is perfect liberty of thought and discussion. The establishment of this liberty may be considered the most valuable achievement of modern civilization, and as a condition of social progress it should be deemed fundamental. The considerations of permanent utility on which it rests must outweigh any calculations of present advantage which from time to time might be thought to demand its violation.

It is evident that this whole argument depends on the assumption that the progress of the race, its intellectual and moral development, is a reality and is valuable. The argument will not appeal to any one who holds with Cardinal Newman that "our race's progress and perfectibility is a dream, because revelation contradicts it"; and he may consistently subscribe to the same writer's conviction that "it would be a gain to this country were it vastly more superstitious, more bigoted, more gloomy, more fierce in its religion, than at present it shows itself to be."

While Mill was writing his brilliant Essay, which every one should read, the English Government of the day (1858) instituted prosecutions for the circulation of the doctrine that it is lawful to put tyrants to death, on the ground that the doctrine is immoral. Fortunately the prosecutions were not persisted in. Mill refers to the matter, and maintains that such a doctrine as tyrannicide (and, let us add, anarchy) does not form any exception to the rule that "there ought to exist the fullest liberty of professing and discussing, as a matter of ethical conviction, any doctrine, however immoral it may be considered."

Exceptions, cases where the interference of the authorities is proper, are only apparent, for they really come under another rule. For instance, if there is a direct instigation to particular acts of violence, there may be a legitimate case for interference. But the incitement must be deliberate and direct. If I write a book condemning existing societies and defending a theory of anarchy, and a man who reads it presently commits an outrage, it may clearly be established that my book made the man an anarchist and induced him to commit the crime, but it would be illegitimate to punish me or suppress the book unless it contained a direct incitement to the specific crime which he committed.

It is conceivable that difficult cases might arise where a government might be strongly tempted, and might be urged by public clamour, to violate the principle of liberty. Let us suppose a case, very improbable, but which will make the issue clear and definite. Imagine that a man of highly magnetic personality, endowed with a wonderful power of infecting others with his own ideas however irrational, in short a typical religious leader, is convinced that the world will come to an end in the course of a few months. He goes about the country preaching and distributing pamphlets; his words have an electrical effect; and the masses of the uneducated and half-educated are persuaded that they have indeed only a few weeks to prepare for the day of Judgment. Multitudes leave their occupations, abandon their work, in order to spend the short time that remains in prayer and listening to the exhortations of the prophet. The country is paralyzed by the gigantic strike; traffic and industries come to a standstill. The people have a perfect legal right to give up their work, and the prophet has a perfect legal right to propagate his opinion that the end of the world is at hand —an opinion which Jesus Christ and his followers in their day held quite as erroneously. It would be said that desperate ills have desperate remedies, and there would be a strong temptation to suppress the fanatic. But to arrest a man who is not breaking the law or exhorting any one to break it, or causing a breach of the peace, would be an act of glaring tyranny. Many will hold that the evil of setting back the clock of liberty would outbalance all the temporary evils, great as they might be, caused by the propagation of a delusion. It would be absurd to deny that liberty of speech may sometimes cause particular harm. Every good thing sometimes does harm. Government, for instance, which makes fatal mistakes; law, which so often bears hardly and inequitably in individual cases. And can the Christians urge any other plea for their religion when they are unpleasantly reminded that it has caused untold suffering by its principle of exclusive salvation?

Once the principle of liberty of thought is accepted as a supreme condition of social progress, it passes from the sphere of ordinary expediency into the sphere of higher expediency which we call justice. In other words it becomes a right on which every man should be able to count. The fact that this right is ultimately based on utility does not justify a government in curtailing it, on the ground of utility, in particular cases.

The recent rather alarming inflictions of penalties for blasphemy in England illustrate this point. It was commonly supposed that the Blasphemy laws (see above, p. 139), though unrepealed, were a dead letter. But since December, 1911, half a dozen persons have been imprisoned for this offence. In these cases Christian doctrines were attacked by poor and more or less uneducated persons in language which may be described as coarse and offensive. Some of the judges seem to have taken the line that it is not blasphemy to attack the fundamental doctrines provided "the decencies of controversy" are preserved, but that "indecent" attacks constitute blasphemy. This implies a new definition of legal blasphemy, and is entirely contrary to the intention of the laws. Sir

J. F. Stephen pointed out that the decisions of judges from the time of Lord Hale (XVIIth century) to the trial of Foote (1883) laid down the same doctrine and based it on the same principle: the doctrine being that it is a crime either to deny the truth of the fundamental doctrines of the Christian religion or to hold them up to contempt or ridicule; and the principle being that Christianity is a part of the law of the land.

The apology offered for such prosecutions is that their object is to protect religious sentiment from insult and ridicule. Sir J. F. Stephen observed: "If the law were really impartial and punished blasphemy only, because it offends the feelings of believers, it ought also to punish such preaching as offends the feelings of unbelievers. All the more earnest and enthusiastic forms of religion are extremely offensive to those who do not believe them." If the law does not in any sense recognize the truth of Christian doctrine, it would have to apply the same rule to the Salvation Army. In fact the law "can be explained and justified only on what I regard as its true principle—the principle of persecution." The opponents of Christianity may justly say: If Christianity is false, why is it to be attacked only in polite language? Its goodness depends on its truth. If you grant its falsehood, you cannot maintain that it deserves special protection. But the law imposes no restraint on the Christian, however offensive his teaching may be to those who do not agree with him; therefore it is not based on an impartial desire to prevent the use of language which causes offence; therefore it is based on the hypothesis that Christianity is true; and therefore its principle is persecution.

Of course, the present administration of the common law in regard to blasphemy does not endanger the liberty of those unbelievers who have the capacity for contributing to progress. But it violates the supreme principle of liberty of opinion and discussion. It hinders uneducated people from saying in the only ways in which they know how to say it, what those who have been brought up differently say, with impunity, far more effectively and far more insidiously. Some of the men who have been imprisoned during the last two years, only uttered in language of deplorable taste views that are expressed more or less politely in books which are in the library of a bishop unless he is a very ignorant person, and against which the law, if it has any validity, ought to have been enforced. Thus the law, as now administered, simply penalizes bad taste and places disabilities upon uneducated freethinkers. If their words offend their audience so far as to cause a disturbance, they should be prosecuted for a breach of public order,[1] not because their words are blasphemous. A man who robs or injures a church, or even an episcopal palace, is not prosecuted for sacrilege, but for larceny or malicious damage or something of the kind.

The abolition of penalties for blasphemy was proposed in the House of Commons (by Bradlaugh) in 1889 and rejected. The reform is urgently needed. It would "prevent the recurrence at irregular intervals of scandalous prosecutions which have never in any one instance benefited any one, least of all the cause which they were intended to serve, and which sometimes afford a channel for the gratification of private malice under the cloak of religion."[2]

The struggle of reason against authority has ended in what appears now to be a decisive and permanent victory for liberty. In the most civilized and progressive countries, freedom of discussion is recognized as a

[1] Blasphemy is an offence in Germany; but it must be proved that offence has actually been given, and the penalty does not exceed imprisonment for three days.

[2] The quotations are from Sir J. F. Stephen's article, "Blasphemy and Blasphemous Libel," in the *Fortnightly Review*, March, 1884, pp. 289–318.

fundamental principle. In fact, we may say
it is accepted as a test of enlightenment, and
the man in the street is forward in acknowl-
edging that countries like Russia and Spain,
where opinion is more or less fettered, must
on that account be considered less civilized
than their neighbours. All intellectual people
who count take it for granted that there is
no subject in heaven or earth which ought
not to be investigated without any deference
or reference to theological assumptions. No
man of science has any fear of publishing
his researches, whatever consequences they
may involve for current beliefs. Criticism
of religious doctrines and of political and social
institutions is free. Hopeful people may feel
confident that the victory is permanent;
that intellectual freedom is now assured to
mankind as a possession for ever; that the
future will see the collapse of those forces
which still work against it and its gradual
diffusion in the more backward parts of the
earth. Yet history may suggest that this
prospect is not assured. Can we be certain
that there may not come a great set-back?
For freedom of discussion and speculation
was, as we saw, fully realized in the Greek
and Roman world, and then an unforeseen
force, in the shape of Christianity, came in
and laid chains upon the human mind and

suppressed freedom and imposed upon man a weary struggle to recover the freedom which he had lost. Is it not conceivable that something of the same kind may occur again? that some new force, emerging from the unknown, may surprise the world and cause a similar set-back?

The possibility cannot be denied, but there are some considerations which render it improbable (apart from a catastrophe sweeping away European culture). There are certain radical differences between the intellectual situation now and in antiquity. The facts known to the Greeks about the nature of the physical universe were few. Much that was taught was not proved. Compare what they knew and what we know about astronomy and geography—to take the two branches in which (besides mathematics) they made most progress. When there were so few demonstrated facts to work upon, there was the widest room for speculation. Now to suppress a number of rival theories in favour of one is a very different thing from suppressing whole systems of established facts. If one school of astronomers holds that the earth goes round the sun, another that the sun goes round the earth, but neither is able to demonstrate its proposition, it is easy for an authority, which has coercive power,

to suppress one of them successfully. But
once it is agreed by all astronomers that the
earth goes round the sun, it is a hopeless
task for any authority to compel men to
accept a false view. In short, because she
is in possession of a vast mass of ascertained
facts about the nature of the universe, reason
holds a much stronger position now than at
the time when Christian theology led her cap-
tive. All these facts are her fortifications.
Again, it is difficult to see what can arrest
the continuous progress of knowledge in
the future. In ancient times this progress
depended on a few; nowadays, many nations
take part in the work. A general conviction of the importance of science prevails
to-day, which did not prevail in Greece.
And the circumstance that the advance of
material civilization depends on science is
perhaps a practical guarantee that scientific
research will not come to an abrupt halt.
In fact science is now a social institution,
as much as religion.

But if science seems pretty safe, it is always
possible that in countries where the scientific
spirit is held in honour, nevertheless, serious
restrictions may be laid on speculations touch-
ing social, political, and religious questions.
Russia has men of science inferior to none,
and Russia has its notorious censorship. It

is by no means inconceivable that in lands
where opinion is now free coercion might be
introduced. If a revolutionary social movement prevailed, led by men inspired by faith
in formulas (like the men of the French
Revolution) and resolved to impose their
creed, experience shows that coercion would
almost inevitably be resorted to. Nevertheless, while it would be silly to suppose that
attempts may not be made in the future
to put back the clock, liberty is in a far more
favourable position now than under the
Roman Empire. For at that time the social
importance of freedom of opinion was not
appreciated, whereas now, in consequence of
the long conflict which was necessary in order
to re-establish it, men consciously realize its
value. Perhaps this conviction will be strong
enough to resist all conspiracies against
liberty. Meanwhile, nothing should be left
undone to impress upon the young that freedom of thought is an axiom of human progress.
It may be feared, however, that this is not
likely to be done for a long time to come.
For our methods of early education are
founded on authority. It is true that children are sometimes exhorted to think for
themselves. But the parent or instructor
who gives this excellent advice is confident
that the results of the child's thinking for

himself will agree with the opinions which his elders consider desirable. It is assumed that he will reason from principles which have already been instilled into him by authority. But if his thinking for himself takes the form of questioning these principles, whether moral or religious, his parents and teachers, unless they are very exceptional persons, will be extremely displeased, and will certainly discourage him. It is, of course, only singularly promising children whose freedom of thought will go so far. In this sense it might be said that "distrust thy father and mother" is the first commandment with promise. It should be a part of education to explain to children, as soon as they are old enough to understand, when it is reasonable, and when it is not, to accept what they are told, on authority.

BIBLIOGRAPHY

General

LECKY, W. E. H., *History of the Rise and Influence of the Spirit of Rationalism in Europe*, 2 vols. (originally published in 1865). WHITE, A. D., *A History of the Warfare of Science with Theology in Christendom*, 2 vols., 1896. ROBERTSON, J. M., *A Short History of Free-thought, Ancient and Modern*, 2 vols., 1906. [Comprehensive, but the notices of the leading freethinkers are necessarily brief, as the field covered is so large. The judgments are always independent.] BENN, A. W., *The History of English Rationalism in the Nineteenth Century*, 2 vols., 1906. [Very full and valuable.]

Greek Thought

GOMPERZ, TH., *Greek Thinkers* (English translation), 4 vols. (1901–12).

English Deists

STEPHEN, LESLIE, *History of English Thought in the Eighteenth Century*, vol. i, 1881.

French Freethinkers of Eighteenth Century

MORLEY, J., *Voltaire; Diderot and the Encyclopædists; Rousseau* (see above, Chapter VI).

Rationalistic Criticism of the Bible (Nineteenth Century)

Articles in *Encyclopædia Biblica*, 4 vols. DUFF, A., *History of Old Testament Criticism*, 1910. CONYBEARE, F. C., *History of New Testament Criticism*, 1910.

Persecution and Inquisition

LEA, H., *A History of the Inquisition of the Middle Ages*, 3 vols., 1888; *A History of the Inquisition of Spain*, 4 vols., 1906. HAYNES, E. S. P., *Religious Persecution*, 1904. For the case of Ferrer see ARCHER, W., *The Life, Trial and Death of Francisco Ferrer*, 1911, and McCABE, J., *The Martyrdom of Ferrer*, 1909.

Toleration

RUFFINI, F., *Religious Liberty* (English translation), 1912. The essays of L. LUZZATTI. *Liberty of Conscience and Science* (Italian), are suggestive.

INDEX

GENERAL HISTORY AND GEOGRAPHY

3. **THE FRENCH REVOLUTION.** By Hilaire Belloc.

4. **A SHORT HISTORY OF WAR AND PEACE.** By G. H. Perris, author of "Russia in Revolution," etc.

7. **MODERN GEOGRAPHY.** By Dr. Marion Newbigin. Shows the relation of physical features to living things and to some of the chief institutions of civilization.

8. **POLAR EXPLORATION.** By Dr. W. S. Bruce, leader of the "Scotia" expedition. Emphasizes the results of the expedition.

13. **MEDIEVAL EUROPE.** By H. W. C. Davis, Fellow at Balliol College, Oxford, author of "Charlemagne," etc.

18. **THE OPENING UP OF AFRICA.** By Sir H. H. Johnston.

19. **THE CIVILIZATION OF CHINA.** By H. A. Giles, Professor of Chinese, Cambridge.

20. **HISTORY OF OUR TIME (1885-1911).** By C. P. Gooch.

22. **THE PAPACY AND MODERN TIMES.** By Rev. William Barry, D.D., author of "The Papal Monarchy," etc. The story of the rise and fall of the Temporal Power.

26. **THE DAWN OF HISTORY.** By J. L. Myers, Professor of Ancient History, Oxford.

30. **ROME.** By W. Warde Fowler, author of "Social Life at Rome," etc.

33. **THE HISTORY OF ENGLAND.** By A. F. Pollard, Professor of English History, University of London.

34. **CANADA.** By A. G. Bradley.

36. **PEOPLES AND PROBLEMS OF INDIA.** By Sir T. W. Holderness. "The best small treatise dealing with the range of subjects fairly indicated by the title."—*The Dial.*

51. **MASTER MARINERS.** By John R. Spears, author of "The History of Our Navy," etc. A history of sea craft adventure from the earliest times.

57. **NAPOLEON.** By H. A. L. Fisher, Vice-Chancellor of Sheffield University. Author of "The Republican Tradition in Europe."

72. **GERMANY OF TO-DAY.** By Charles Tower.

76. **THE OCEAN. A GENERAL ACCOUNT OF THE SCIENCE OF THE SEA.** By Sir John Murray, K. C. B., Naturalist H. M. S. "Challenger," 1872-1876, joint author of "The Depths of the Ocean," etc.

78. **LATIN AMERICA.** By William R. Shepherd, Professor of History, Columbia. With maps. The historical, artistic and commercial development of the Central South American republics.

THE HOME UNIVERSITY
LIBRARY *of Modern Knowledge*

Edited by Professors J. Arthur Thomson, Gilbert Murray, H. A. L. Fisher and W. T. Brewster.

Comprehensive and authoritative volumes on every prominent educational and cultural subject. The books are cloth bound, printed on high grade paper, with bibliographies, indices, and illustrations, charts and maps where needed. Jackets in two colors. Each volume complete and sold separately. *Per volume,* **One Dollar.**

(ORDER BY NUMBER)

AMERICAN HISTORY

[*Order Number*]

25. **THE CIVIL WAR (1854-1865). By Frederick L. Paxson,** Professor of American History, University of Wisconsin.

39. **RECONSTRUCTION AND UNION (1865-1912). By Paul Leland Haworth.** A History of the United States in our own times.

47. **THE COLONIAL PERIOD (1607-1766). By Charles McLean Andrews,** Professor of American History, Yale.

67. **FROM JEFFERSON TO LINCOLN (1815-1860). By William MacDonald,** Professor of History, Brown University. The author makes the history of this period circulate about constitutional ideas and slavery sentiment.

82. **THE WARS BETWEEN ENGLAND AND AMERICA (1763-1815). By Theodore C. Smith,** Professor of American History, Williams College. A history of the period, with especial emphasis on The Revolution and The War of 1812.

84. **THE GROWTH OF EUROPE.** By **Granville Cole,** Professor of Geology, Royal College of Science, Ireland. A study of the geology and physical geography in connection with the political geography.

86. **EXPLORATION OF THE ALPS.** By **Arnold Lunn, M.A.**

92. **THE ANCIENT EAST.** By **D. G. Hogarth, M. A., F. B. A., F. S. A.** Connects with Prof. Myers's "Dawn of History" (No. 26) at about 1000 B. C. and reviews the history of Assyria, Babylon, Cilicia, Persia and Macedonia.

94. **THE NAVY AND SEA POWER.** By **David Hannay,** author of "Short History of the Royal Navy," etc. A brief history of the navies, sea power, and ship growth of all nations, including the rise and decline of America on the sea, and explaining the present British supremacy.

95. **BELGIUM.** By **R. C. K. Ensor,** sometime Scholar of Balliol College. The geographical, linguistic, historical, artistic and literary associations.

100. **POLAND.** By **J. Alison Phillips,** University of Dublin. The history of Poland with special emphasis upon the Polish question of the present day.

102. **SERBIA.** By **L. F. Waring,** with preface by **J. M. Jovanovitch,** Serbian Minister to Great Britain. The main outlines of Serbian history, with special emphasis on the immediate causes of the war and the questions in the after-the-war settlement.

104. **OUR FORERUNNERS.** By **M. C. Burkitt, M.A., F.S.A.** A comprehensive study of the beginnings of mankind and the culture of the prehistoric era.

105. **COMMERCIAL GEOGRAPHY.** By **Marion I. Newbigin.** Fundamental conceptions of commodities, transport and market.

108. **WALES.** By **W. Watkin Davies, M.A., F.R. Hist. S.,** Barrister-at-Law, author of "How to Read History," etc.

110. **EGYPT.** By **E. A. Wallis Budge, M.A., Litt. D.**

LITERATURE AND ART

2. **SHAKESPEARE.** By **John Masefield.** "One of the very few indispensable adjuncts to a Shakespearian Library."—*Boston Transcript.*

27. **MODERN ENGLISH LITERATURE.** By **G. H. Mair.** From Wyatt and Surrey to Synge and Yeats. "One of the best of this great series." —*Chicago Evening Post.*

31. **LANDMARKS IN FRENCH LITERATURE.** By **G. L. Strachey,** Scholar of Trinity College, Cambridge. "It is difficult to imagine how a better account of French Literature could be given in 250 pages."—*London Times.*

43. **MATTER AND ENERGY.** By F. Soddy, Lecturer in Physical Chemistry and Radioactivity, University of Glasgow. "Brilliant. Can hardly be surpassed. Sure to attract attention."—*New York Sun.*

53. **ELECTRICITY.** By Gisbert Kapp, Professor of Electrical Engineering, University of Birmingham.

54. **THE MAKING OF THE EARTH.** By J. W. Gregory, Professor of Geology, Glasgow University. 38 maps and figures. Describes the origin of the earth, the formation and changes of its surface and structure, its geological history, the first appearance of life, and its influence upon the globe.

56. **MAN: A HISTORY OF THE HUMAN BODY.** By A. Keith, M.D., Hunterian Professor, Royal College of Surgeons, London. Shows how the human body developed.

63. **THE ORIGIN AND NATURE OF LIFE.** By Benjamin M. Moore, Professor of Bio-Chemistry, Liverpool.

68. **DISEASE AND ITS CAUSES.** By W. T. Councilman, M.D., LL.D., Professor of Pathology, Harvard University.

71. **PLANT LIFE.** By J. B. Farmer, D.Sc., F.R.S., Professor of Botany in the Imperial College of Science, London. This very fully illustrated volume contains an account of the salient features of plant form and function.

74. **NERVES.** By David Fraser Harris, M.D., Professor of Physiology, Dalhousie University, Halifax. Explains in nontechnical language the place and powers of the nervous system.

85. **SEX.** By J. Arthur Thomson and Patrick Geddes, joint authors of "The Evolution of Sex."

90. **CHEMISTRY.** By Raphael Meldola, F.R.S., Professor of Chemistry, Finsbury Technical College. Presents the way in which the science has developed and the stage it has reached.

111. **BIOLOGY.** By J. Arthur Thomson and Patrick Geddes.

112. **BACTERIOLOGY.** By Prof. Carl H. Browning.

PHILOSOPHY AND RELIGION

35. **THE PROBLEMS OF PHILOSOPHY.** By Bertrand Russell, Lecturer and Late Fellow Trinity College, Cambridge.

44. **BUDDHISM.** By Mrs. Rhys Davids, Lecturer on Indian Philosophy, Manchester.

46. **ENGLISH SECTS: A HISTORY OF NONCONFORMITY.** By W. B. Selbie, Principal of Manchester College, Oxford.

50. **THE MAKING OF THE NEW TESTAMENT.** By B. W. Bacon, Professor of New Testament Criticism, Yale. An authoritative summary of the results of modern critical research with regard to the origins of the New Testament.

52. **ETHICS.** By G. E. Moore, Lecturer in Moral Science, Cambridge. Discusses what is right and what is wrong, and the whys and wherefores.

55. **MISSIONS: THEIR RISE AND DEVELOPMENT.** By Mrs. Mandell Creighton, author of "History of England." The author seeks to prove that missions have done more to civilize the world than any other human agency.

60. **COMPARATIVE RELIGION.** By Prof. J. Estlin Carpenter. "One of the few authorities on this subject compares all the religions to see what they have to offer on the great themes of religion."— *Christian Work and Evangelist.*

65. **THE LITERATURE OF THE OLD TESTAMENT.** By George F. Moore, Professor of the History of Religion, Harvard University. "A popular work of the highest order. Will be profitable to anybody who cares enough about Bible study to read a serious book on the subject."— *American Journal of Theology.*

69. **A HISTORY OF FREEDOM OF THOUGHT.** By John B. Bury, M.A., LL.D., Regius Professor of Modern History in Cambridge University. Summarizes the history of the long struggle between authority and reason and of the emergence of the principle that coercion of opinion is a mistake.

88. **RELIGIOUS DEVELOPMENT BETWEEN OLD AND NEW TESTAMENTS.** By R. H. Charles, Canon of Westminster. Shows how religious and ethical thought between 180 B. C. and 100 A. D. grew naturally into that of the New Testament.

96. **A HISTORY OF PHILOSOPHY.** By Clement C. J. Webb, Oxford.

SOCIAL SCIENCE

1. **PARLIAMENT. ITS HISTORY, CONSTITUTION, AND PRACTICE.** By Sir Courtenay P. Ilbert, Clerk of the House of Commons.

5. **THE STOCK EXCHANGE.** By F. W. Hirst, Editor of the London *Economist.* Reveals to the nonfinancial mind the facts about investment, speculation, and the other terms which the title suggests.

6. **IRISH NATIONALITY.** By Mrs. J. R. Green. A brilliant account of the genius and mission of the Irish people. "An entrancing work, and I would advise everyone with a drop of Irish blood in his veins or a vein of Irish sympathy in his heart to read it."— *New York Times Review.*

10. **THE SOCIALIST MOVEMENT.** By J. Ramsay Macdonald, Chairman of the British Labor Party.

11. **THE SCIENCE OF WEALTH.** By J. A. Hobson, author of "Problems of Poverty." A study of the structure and working of the modern business world.

Published by

HENRY HOLT AND COMPANY, 19 West 44th St., New York